Twenty Something in the Twenty Something's

by
Jeffrey Moore

1663 Liberty Drive, Suite 200
Bloomington, Indiana 47403
(800) 839-8640
www.AuthorHouse.com

© 2005 Jeffrey Moore. All Rights Reserved.

No part of this book may be reproduced, stored in a retrieval system, or transmitted by any means without the written permission of the author.

First published by AuthorHouse 10/31/05

ISBN: 1-4208-7631-7 (sc)
ISBN: 1-4208-7630-9 (dj)

Library of Congress Control Number: 2005907254

Printed in the United States of America
Bloomington, Indiana

This book is printed on acid-free paper.

Dedications

To my big brother, Craig, who didn't have to, but did: You may not even realize it, but you gave me the greatest gift anyone could ever give me. I can never fully thank you or ever repay you for the countless number of hours of your life that you shared with me. My only hope is that I can one day do for someone what you did for me.

To the Bellamy family: Thank you for being there when it really counted and for showing me what true friendship is all about.

To my good friend, Conrad, who truly holds the world in his hands, but just hasn't realized it yet.

To Johnny T, probably my oldest friend, the easiest person to talk to, and the reason why I can no longer drink white wine! One of my greatest fears is losing your friendship, buddy.

To Brent: You may not realize it, but that tennis racket meant more to me than you would probably think. It showed me just what kind of friend you truly are. PS: I will beat you, eventually.

To Frank and Claudia: Thank you for always welcoming me into your home and offering me a place at your dinner table.

To my sister, who always reminded me when doing something a little shady that I'm so much better than that. Also thank you for all the work you did on this book, this book is not possible with out you.

To my Magna family, who made an unbearable two years bearable!

To Magna, for laying me off and giving me the opportunity to write this book! It's funny how things work out!

To Saunders: Don't sell yourself short, hommie. You are one of the smartest people I know. Don't waste big potential on small things.

To Katie Tompkins: You were the greatest tutor I could have ever asked for. I always considered you a big sister, even if you didn't know it.

To Leanne Foti, whose passing words of inspiration kept me focused on finishing this book!

To Eryn: Thank you for inspiring me and re-awakening me.

To Booter: Although we have grown so far apart, I still consider you a brother.

To Katrina, who didn't have to forgive me, but did: You have taught me the true lesson of forgiveness.

To Jordan: You were always a true friend and I hate the way our friendship ended. I only hope that one day we can be as close as we once were.

To Mr. Williamson: You were the best coach I ever had. Thank you for never allowing me to do anything but my best.

To the Bootlands and Hayes families: Thank you for giving me the second home when I so badly needed it, and thanks to you, Poppa Booter, for saying I was doing nothing with my life. Those words stuck with me and have forced me to prove you wrong.

To Vee, who was the most giving person I have ever met: I'm sorry for never being the friend I should have been.

To Joanne: You were the first person I ever let read my work. Thank you for giving me the confidence to do this.

To Big Mo: It's only now that I get what you were trying so hard to tell me about self-respect. Holla at your boy.

To L'il Mo: I will never be able to think about Kingston without thinking about you.

To Palmer: You are the best wingman in the business and one of the funniest people I know.

To Barberella: Though our friendship has had more ups and downs than a roller coaster, I can't imagine not having you in my life.

To David Forbes: I can't think of anyone I would rather share lunch break with than you.

To Pete Sandhu, my brother from another mother: Thank you for everything. Thank you for taking me under your wing. Thank you for always providing me with a job whenever I needed it. Most of all, thank you for being my friend.

To the rest of the Sandhu family: Thank you for always making me feel like I was one of you.

To Brent Playter: Thank you for not firing a clumsy kid and for being my big brother at work. "You betcha!"

To all my Bradford High teachers, who always told me I had the ability to do something special with my life, especially: Mrs. Tompkins, Mrs. Begin, Mrs. Bogardis, Ms. Bridgman, Ms. Jarrett (who is pretty), Ms. Clubine, Mr. Kennedy (you spud), Mr. Nickol (the best math teacher in the world), Mrs. Padykula, Mr. Shank, Mr. Stephens, Ms. Gray

(Mrs. A) and to you, Mr. Walker: Thank you for putting up with more nonsense than any student should ever give to a teacher.

To Kyle (a.k.a. Kellogg): You have always been my friend, even when I probably didn't deserve it. Thank you, Kellogg, I mean that.

To Jenn and Kristen Marks: Thank you for being my extended sisters in life.

To the Moore family: Thank you for the unconditional love.

To the Gagne family: I wish we could have stayed in touch.

To my extended family, especially Blair, Roz, Eddie Launch-like-a-rocket, Modo, Jerry, Doyle, my cuz Lebert, O-Dogg, Washington, Baggs, Colin, Mario, Cory, Shaw, Brain cell (Megan Christie), Trish the dish, Havie, Teo Mossa (from my Panama Crew), Fred, Perry, Daryl, Jenn Hall, Jenn Harbridge, Arudabaker, Lopes, Kathryn Pal"moore", Poxan (back in the day brother): Thank you guys for always keeping it so fun.

To Megan Hayes: thank you for standing by me side threw my roughest years.

To Ash: Im sorry I let the drugs get in the way of our friendship.

To Kerry: Kelly Interior design school starts in September (hint, hint).

To my father: I wish we had a relationship that was more than just calls on Christmas and birthdays. I know I will make the effort but I can't do it alone.

To the most important and influential person in my life, the person who sacrificed more for me than anyone should have to: Thank you for always believing in me, even when they wanted to kick me out of school or when the police would come knocking at our door. I will never forget how hard you tried for me, and it's only now I can appreciate how much you had on your plate. I will always remember our basketball games together. You had the hardest job in the world and you always made it look easy. In case you are still wondering, Mom, I'm talking about you. I know I don't say it often enough, but I do love you. Thank you for always being my guiding light when my world becomes cloudy. Looking at Sarah, I feel it's safe to say you did one hell of a job. I have all the admiration and respect in the world for you. I love you and, most of all, this book is for you.

To all of the people I mentioned: This book would not be possible without you. Thank you for sharing a part of your life with me. I truly feel I'm the luckiest person in the world for being able to know all of you.

"We discover ourselves through others."
-Carl Jung

Introduction

First things first
I honestly have no idea how I graduated high school, and I have even less of a clue on how I ever got accepted into college (especially into the Police Foundations program). In high school, while other people were learning math or English, I was out in the school parking lot, getting hammered or high.

My only focus in college was "How am I going to get high? Then, how am I going to get drunk, and finally, who I am going to sleep with tonight?"

To some of you, this may sound like a lot of fun. But the truth was, I had become a complete waste, and worst of all, I was a wrecking ball in the lives of people who cared for me the most. I sold drugs to get high, I worked to get drunk, and I lied to get laid. I would wake up in the morning, hung over, having no idea how I had gotten home, or who was lying next to me. I find it absolutely fascinating, when I look back and think that this is what I thought life was all about. I remember waking up one morning after spending all my grocery and rent money at the bar.

I was forced to eat three-day-old fries out of a Taco Bell bag. I remember eating those fries and thinking, **"What am I doing with my life?"** I wanted to exit this world that I had created.

I had become extremely sick and tired of being in last place, when I knew I had first-place potential.

The importance of that brief overview of my life is that I want you to see where I am coming from with this book. I'm not some rich millionaire's son who's trying to preach to you about becoming successful, yet has no idea what it feels like to be broke and lost, with no future.

I wrote this book because I am sick of people who have never lived that life trying to preach to those who are. I wrote this book because as I searched for the answers that I was looking for in life, I noticed that I was not the only one struggling. I wrote this book in hopes of being a voice to the ones who are just like the person I used to be. This book is dedicated to people who are in their twenties and struggling to find answers as they enter true adulthood. With that being said, if you, the reader, do not fit into this age demographic, please do not put down this book. There are extremely important lessons taught throughout this book that can apply to any life, regardless of age.

> *"I am committed to living my life to the fullest, by not judging and dwelling on my past, but by living for a commitment to being the best I can be in the future."*
> *- Jeffrey Moore*

TABLE OF CONTENTS

Dedications v

Introduction xi

Chapter 1 3
The realization that your domino effect start right now
Workshop 1 12

Chapter 2 17
The second domino and the beginning of momentum
Workshop 2 30

Chapter 3 33
Television and the Media, the nasty trick they have pulled on us
Workshop 3 41

Chapter 4 44
The Devil hiding out in our wallet
Workshop 4 53

Chapter 5 56
The key to success is to surround your self with it
Workshop 5 65

Chapter 6 68
Fear the other four letter word that starts with F
Workshop 6 75

Chapter 7 78
Procrastination and Goals sitting on both sides of the teeter-totter
Workshop 7 91

Chapter 8 .... *94*

The final push getting naked with you and the 6 fundamentals towards achieving success

Workshop 8 .... *110*

Twenty-Something in the Twenty-Something's

Chapter 1
Introduction and the Realization That Your Domino Effect Starts Right Now, If You Want

"We do not remember days; we remember moments."
-Cesar Pareso

My First Words...
When it comes to life, especially this particular period of life, I'm reminded of Charles Dickens's most famous quote from *A Tale of Two Cities:* "It was the best of times, it was the worst of times, it was the age of wisdom, it was the age of foolishness, it was the epoch of belief, it was the epoch of incredulity, it was the season of Light, it was the season of Darkness, it was the spring of hope, it was the winter of despair, we had everything before us, we had nothing before us..."

I don't think I could possibly describe it any better. How else can you explain this period of life that we all go through? How else can you possibly explain the absolute feeling of chaos that comes with age?

Realization
It hit me like a cold and hard slap to the face. There it was, lying right in front of me, the truth that I had been trying so hard not to see:

I was twenty-two years old. I had no idea what career I wanted, I barely had a job, and I was living at home with my mom. I know this may sound silly, but when I was much younger, I always envisioned myself being so much further ahead at this early stage of life!

I was petrified with the thought that I was a failure. I was frustrated and fed up with being scared of being scared. My head was clouded and I lacked focus. I would sit and listen in complete fascination and personal frustration, as people I knew seemed to be so much further ahead in life than I was.

I just wished I could make up my mind on what direction to take my life. I wished I was already forty. That way, I could just be living the life I wanted, not having any idea of how I got there. If I was forty, I wouldn't have to deal with that one question, the question that has kept me up at night, tossing and turning, just wishing I had the answer to. No matter where I went, the question seemed to follow me. The question: "What am I going to do with my life?"

The First Push
Welcome to the next chapter in your life. The final words have been written on your adolescence. You are no longer a worry-free teenager whose biggest problem is what table to sit at in the lunchroom cafeteria. The Friday night house parties are gone and have been replaced with a growing sense of responsibility. The once-large clique that you associated with has been whittled down to a few people. Some, you thought, would be there and some you didn't. Welcome to the first stages of adulthood. Change is a frightening thing to deal with, especially one of this magnitude.

You are now facing an endless road of decisions that you will be forced to make. While it is true that you could try hard to stay where you are, you know it will only lead to failure. This is absolutely the most amazingly scary and interesting part of life that I have lived to date. I have found it more than interesting as I watch the change, of not just myself, but everyone else around me.

Things will never be the same when you come to the realization that you, much like myself, are just twenty-something in the twenty-something's!

> *"I once was blind, but now I see."*
> *- Amazing Grace*

Dominos Changed My Life!
I would like to introduce you to an analogy that has changed my life and will help to change yours.

Life is one giant domino effect! Do you remember when you were much younger and you would play dominos? Oh-so-very carefully, one by one, you would stand the dominos up before giving that first domino a little push and watching as they all fell down. This game that children all around the world play every day has now become my metaphor for life.

If you read the introduction to this book, then you have already learned a little about who I used to be.

This book was created from the understanding that we create the life that we live by choosing the dominos that we knock over. For instance, you can't knock over the domino effect of a life with an STD without first deciding to knock over the domino of unprotected sex.

Before I understood the analogy of the domino effect, my life was going nowhere. I had just been laid off of my job, I was freshly kicked out of college, and the future seemed bleak, at best. Then I had my epiphany: If I wanted to, I could change my life...today! If I wanted to be successful, I could! All I had to do was start making different decisions and actions with my life. All I had to do was start knocking over positive dominos instead of negative ones. All I had to do was create a new momentum in my life.

It was my decision: I could continue the present self-destructing domino effect I was used to, or, I could stop it and start a new one by knocking over that first domino in the right direction.

> *"In the long run, we shape our own lives and we shape ourselves. The process never ends until we die. And the choices we make are ultimately our own responsibility"*
> *- Eleanor Roosevelt*

The First Domino
Who are you? It's an interesting question, isn't it?

In the process of this book we will touch upon this question several times, but for right now, stop and think about it: Who are you, exactly?

When you look in the mirror, do you recognize your own reflection?

A very close friend of mine was in a horrific car accident when she was younger. Consequently, she suffered a case of amnesia. She actually looked in the mirror and did not know who she was. I don't know what that would feel like, but I do imagine it would be quite scary. I also imagine it might be quite liberating. If you have no idea who you are, how can you possibly know what you are capable of doing? The possibilities are endless!

> *"You can do anything you set your mind to."*
> *- Eminem*

Often in life, we sabotage ourselves by not living as what we are, but rather living as what we *think* we are. A lot of people I know are complete zombies to what true potential they have. There are many reasons for this, most noticeably, past failures or parents' and friends' beliefs. A lot of our traits and beliefs, whether we realize it or not, are shaped by our parents and friends. *"We are what we surround ourselves with.*" I actually know people who, since the age of one second, have been told that they will become a doctor, a lawyer, or a professional athlete when they grow up. Usually, this is because their parents have always dreamed that they would become these things themselves, but somewhere along the path of life, they became lost and wound up becoming who they are today. If there is one thing that I want to make very clear, it is that **this is your life**. So why try to live someone else's dream?

I know someone whose father's ultimate dream was to play in the NHL, but due to a lack of skill, he never made it. The father turned his own pain of a lost dream into a driving force to get his son to live the dream he never could. This over-controlling father would force his son to shoot five hundred pucks a day, regardless if he was sick or had schoolwork. My friend wasn't even allowed to clean his room until he was done his daily chore of shooting. I am a strong believer in parents helping to develop their children's natural talents and helping them to learn the importance of a strong work ethic, but there was a line crossed here. What happened is that my friend began to have a growing resentment towards his father, which in turn carried over into hockey. While many kids his age were enjoying the game, he associated the feeling of playing hockey the same way you may associate cutting the grass, or taking out the trash: hockey had become a chore. The last time I spoke to my friend, he hadn't played hockey in two years (or talked to his father in three years).

> *"Adults are always asking kids what they want to be when they grow up 'cause they're trying to get ideas!"*
> - Paula Poundstone

The Only Person to Ask Is You
Here's a very important question that you need to ask yourself. What is it that you truly love to do?

Not what your parents have told you to love, but what do you *truly* love to do?

If you're going to school to become a doctor, but your true passion is playing the piano or acting, who are you cheating? If you want to be a female mechanic, but you're studying cosmetology, then who are you truly letting down? If you're not chasing after your true burning desire, what are you chasing, besides someone else's dream and a life without fulfillment?

Remember, this little thing called life is yours and no one else's. It's not your mom's, it's not your dad's, and it's definitely not one of your friend's; it is *yours*!

No one but you has to wake up every day and be you, and no one but you knows how it feels to be you. So always make sure in life that you are true to yourself.

> *"Few is the number of those who think with their own minds and feel with their own hearts."*
> *-Albert Einstein*

Bill's Formula for Failure!
A very good friend of mine, who we will call Bill, once said something that, if followed, will cause an unrewarding life — I guarantee it. It was, "Hey, it's work. It's not supposed to be fun. If it was fun they would have called it fun, and not work." Where did he learn this pessimistic point of view? Growing up, he would ask his father about his job and would always be given this same response: "Hey, it's work. It's not supposed to be fun. If it was fun, they would have called it fun and not work."

> *"Most men would feel insulted if it were proposed to employ them in throwing stones over a wall, and then throwing them back again, merely that they might earn wages. But many are no more worthily employed now."*
> *-Henry David Thoreau*

I asked Bill where his father worked and quickly learned that the notion of "work can't be fun" had been passed on through several generations of unhappy factory workers teaching their sons this so-called lesson in life. The men in his family had been working at the same factory for over fifty years! One generation after another, much like a domino effect. Now it was his time to continue the cycle. Bill had just started working with his father and was already hating his job and finding his life to have become very lackluster. When I questioned Bill about why he didn't go to school to study fashion (which was his true passion and calling in life), he told me that his father said, "Fashion is for fags and women." Bill was suffering from a severe lack of self-belief and a strong case of parental control.

I am willing to make a bold prediction of what the future holds for Bill. Bill will marry his high school sweetheart and she will become pregnant within the first two years of marriage. Thus, he will be forced to work at the factory for the rest of his life. He will hate his job and feel trapped. As their dreams pass them by, feelings of resentment will build between Bill and his wife. The tiny quirks they used to find cute about each other, like Bill's funny noises he makes when eating, or Sabrina's inability to blow her nose without waking up the neighbours, have now become the things they find most annoying about each other.

He will count down the days until the weekend, essentially counting down the wasted days of his life, and they will both spend more time thinking about what could have and should have been, instead of what is. Before he knows it, he's telling his son, "Hey, it's work. It's not supposed to be fun. If it was fun, they would have called it fun, and not work."

Does this sound like any one you know?

I sometimes can't believe that I actually know people who live like this. It's sad, but true. So if this is your dream life, then continue to follow the pattern that Bill has shown us. But if you imagine something different for yourself, you better start now! It's amazing how something like a job can cause such a strong domino effect in your life.

Wake Up And Smell Your Potential!
All too often, we allow success and our dream life to pass through our hands, without even knowing it. This happens because we never believe that we can actually accomplish something as great as living our dream.

I want to make something very clear: This book is only the first push in your domino effect. You will not be a millionaire at the conclusion of the final page. Nor will you be living the life you have always dreamed of when you close the book for the last time. However, what you will have done is planted the seed. You have opened yourself up, and are now prepared to grow.

"When the student is ready, the teacher will appear."
- Ancient Asian Proverb

Remember: The longer we decide to not believe we can do something, the less time there is to do it.

Keynotes to remember for Chapter 1

- Life is one giant domino effect.

- You are ultimately the person who will choose which dominos to knock over, so choose wisely.

- Always make sure that you are following your heart, and are not trying to live someone else's dreams.

- Many of our beliefs are shaped through our parents and friends.

- This little thing called life is yours and no one else's. It's not your mom's, it's not your dad's, and it's definitely not one of your friend's; it is *yours*! No one but you has to wake up every day and be you, and no one but you knows how it feels to be you.

Quote to Remember

> *"Few is the number of those who think with their own minds and feel with their own hearts."*
> *- Albert Einstein*

Workshop 1
The first push…

Workshop 1

Creating the First Push in a Positive Domino Effect
Welcome to the first of eight very important workshops. Welcome to the push that can change your life. A very important note should be made right now by you, the reader. This book is a great tool for reshaping and defining your life. However, if you are not 110 percent committed to changing your life, right now, then I am sorry, but this book is not for you. If you want to get the most out of this book, I strongly recommend that you buy a blank notebook and use it as you work through this book. Use the notebook to complete the exercises that I have outlined for you at the end of each chapter. It will help you to keep organized and track your progress. You can also keep track of personal thoughts and accomplishments along the way.

Remember, the first real step towards making a change is the desire to change. Studies have shown that only 10 percent of people who purchase this (or any other book) will read past the first chapter. So, if you are not committed to changing your life today, then join the other 90 percent and never open this book again. When you are ready to create a domino effect for success in your life, I will still be here waiting for you. This book isn't for those who prefer to stand on the sidelines.

It's extremely important that you not skip these workshops and that you do them immediately after the chapter, while your brain is still warm. Your brain is no different than any muscle in your body. It needs to be warmed up before it is able to reach its peak potential. You wouldn't run a marathon without stretching and warming up first. So why would you brainstorm without warming up your brain? The chapter you have just read is, in my opinion, the equivalent of a ten-minute stretch and jog.

Exercise 1
I want you to grab a pen and your notebook to create a list for the following three topics.
What are you currently unsatisfied with in life?
What could be better?
What would you like to change?

When I first did this exercise, I made a goal of listing off at least 100 things in my life that I was unsatisfied with. I listed off everything from feeling lazy and unmotivated, to money and personal relationships. Anything that I was not 100 percent satisfied with, I listed. I believe it took me around a half hour. I know this may sound like a lot of work, but if you don't know everything that you are unsatisfied with in life, then how are you ever going to change it? By listing off everything you are unsatisfied with, you are giving yourself a reference to one day look back on and say, "I can't believe I used to live that way!"

Exercise 2
Now that you have become more aware of what it is in life that you are unsatisfied with, pick the top ten things on that list that keep you up at night, and let's figure out together how to solve these issues. If one of the things you are unsatisfied with is always being broke, examine when it is you feel the poorest and what actions you're taking daily towards continuing this feeling.

What you may not realize is that the things you are most frustrated with in life are actually created through your every day actions. Remember, the person you are today didn't just happen overnight. Your every day actions have led to the domino effect that you are currently on. You are not a victim but rather a creation of your own self.

> *"My doctor said I would have less nosebleeds if I just kept my finger out of there."*
> - Ralph Wiggum

After choosing the top ten things that you are currently unsatisfied with in life, I want you to take a blank page and divide it into three columns. At the top of column one, write in "Problem." At the top of column two, write in "Where will this take my life," and finally at the top of the third column, write in "Solution." Underneath the first (or "Problem") column, write in those ten elements of life you are currently unsatisfied with. In the second column, which is a very important column, write in how this problem will affect your life. Essentially, what walls is this problem going to create towards restricting your life's possibilities? For instance, someone who gambles a lot and is sick of wasting away all of their hard-earned money might fill in "Not changing this part of my life may force me to become broke and lose my significant other or friends." What is this ultimately going to cost you if you don't rid yourself of it immediately? Use this as a motivating factor for finding a solution. Now, in the last column create a solution for this. Someone with a gambling problem may choose to join Gamblers Anonymous, or at least stop going to casinos.

To every question, there is an answer. You know what the problem is; find out how to rid yourself of it. If it's a personal relationship that wears you down, learn to say good-bye. If it's a job you hate, find a job you think you might enjoy, and begin taking steps towards getting it. If it's being overweight, get up and join a gym or Weight Watchers. Knock over that first domino in ridding your life of this problem. Push that first domino down with authority and passion. **Begin to reshape your life right now!** Create a change by looking at what you stand to lose. Once you see what you stand to lose, it should motivate you beyond your procrastination and force you to find a solution. When I found what I stood to lose, I couldn't sit down for another second. I had to create the solution to my problems. There was simply too much at stake for me to waste another millisecond on my old, self-destructive domino effect.

There is no reason for why you can't eliminate these stresses from your life.

> *"Life ultimately means taking responsibility to find the right answers to its problems and to fulfill the tasks which it constantly sets for each individual."*
> *- Viktor E. Frankl*

Exercise 3

Over the duration of this book, I will be asking you to do many exercises. This exercise is going to help you organize your day so that you can become more efficient with your time.

I call this exercise, "A self-meeting a day helps to keep procrastination away." (I like things that rhyme.) This seemingly small activity is really going to help you get your day off to a bang, and all it takes is fifteen minutes. I usually do it first thing in the morning with my breakfast and tea. I take out my notebook and I write down everything I need to do, from most important to least important. Then, I work out a rough schedule of my day, and see how I am going to be able to accomplish everything that needs to be done. As I accomplish something, I cross it off. At the end of the night before I go to bed, I look back at my schedule. I take note of not only what was accomplished, but also, what wasn't. Becoming organized and time-efficient helps to eliminate needless stress, and more importantly, it makes sure you do what needs to be done.

This is the conclusion of Chapter 1. So, what you need to decide is are you going to be in that 10 percent who follow through with continuing to the next chapter, or are you going to join the 90 percent who will never gain the knowledge that this book contains?

Chapter 2
The Second Domino and the Beginning of Momentum

*"Every decision you make indicates
what you believe you are worth."*
-*A Course in Miracles*

Decisions, Decisions
If there is one thing in life we can count on, it is that a brand new day will undoubtedly bring brand new decisions. When these new decisions are mixed in with all of our old, unfinished decisions that yesterday left behind, sometimes life's decisions can seem a little overwhelming.

Thinking Way Too Much
When it comes to the extremely important decisions that everyone must face in life, there seems to be a constant quote that I have caught, not only myself, but also many others, saying as well. The quote is, "If I just knew what the right decision was, I would make it!" The quote is usually followed with days of sitting on the couch with semi-contemplation, followed with days of whining to co-workers and friends, until the decision is made *for* you.

If this sounds at all like you, then pay close attention, because I have some important news for you, the reader. When it comes to life's decisions, there are no wrong decisions! That's right. You read that correctly. Whatever decision you make on any topic is the right one.

You can't make a wrong decision. You are probably reading this and thinking that I have gone completely insane. After all, if you hadn't made that one silly decision, your life would be so much better off, right? Stop and think for one second: Because of that decision, what have you learned? What are you more aware of in life now? What have you learned that has helped you to become stronger and more in touch with yourself? Stop looking at setbacks in such a narrow and negative way. Life is about learning. There are no mistakes, just lessons learned.

This is so important to remember, because as long as you are following your heart and what you feel is in the total best interest for yourself and others, then there is no wrong decision when it comes to life. There are, however, poor decisions and we will cover those later.

Every decision you have made, unwillingly or not, has helped to create who you are. So if you don't like who you are now, take a look at the decisions you are constantly making.

> *"If you don't make a decision about how you're going to live, then you have already made a decision, haven't you?"*
> *-Tony Robbins*

The Math of Decisions
There is a math involved with making decisions; it is the math that creates not only the domino effect of our lives, but also the domino effect of our world. The math is very simple and easy to understand:

$$\text{Decision} = \text{actions} = \text{results}.$$

There can be no results in life without a decision. Ultimately, the result of your life is based on the decisions you make. In the final chapter, I will introduce you to the six fundamentals that will change your life. This math is a major component of the fundamentals. The only reason anyone has accomplished something in life that you haven't is because they have decided to do something, whereas you only thought about it.

Decisions involve commitment and actions. Thoughts involve nothing. I am going to say that one more time so it's crystal clear. **Decisions involve commitment and actions. Thoughts involve nothing.** Just because you have thought about something does not mean you have made a decision, nor does it mean that anything will come from this thought. On the other hand, once you have made a decision and a commitment to sticking with this decision, actions will follow which in turn creates a result on some level.

The biggest difference in life between the great achievers and the unsuccessful is the difference in their drive and dedication towards making and committing to their decisions. The reason you are exactly who you are today, is simply because you have decided to be that person. You have decided that the way you live is good enough for you. You have decided that you are worth everything that you are right now. If you want more from life, all you have to do is decide to get it. Make a decision and then a commitment towards that decision. And by this I mean, no matter what happens, no matter what first results you get, you are going to stick with this decision until you get what you want. Whatever it is you want in life, it is only a decision away!

Career Path
In the last chapter, I talked about Bill, who had decided to listen to his dad (and not his heart) when it came to the career he wanted.

As I mentioned in the last chapter, without a doubt, the number one theme that seems to be present with my generation is a sense of confusion and frustration when deciding what career path to follow.

When I was facing the decision of choosing a career, I felt an extreme sense of urgency. It was like my head was on fire and if I didn't decide what career I was going to choose right now, my world was going to blow up. If this sounds like you, my first advice is to relax and drop your stress level. You are only hurting yourself by freaking out and not focusing on what is really at hand. When solving a problem, especially one this large, you must spend 10 percent of your time on the problem and 90 percent of your time on the solution.

My Answer for Choosing a Career!
In my opinion, the most important thing to do when choosing a career is to become proactive with what you love. That's it!

If you want to know what job to do for the rest of your life, decide to be proactive with what you love. You may be sitting there saying, "What the heck is that supposed to mean?" If you were expecting me to suggest something else like, "Pick a career that pays well, but isn't very rewarding," then maybe you got this book confused with a book that gives bad advice. The following quote might help to shed a little light on my answer.

> *"This is the beginning of a new day.*
> *You have been given this day to use as you will.*
> *You can waste it or use it for good.*
> *What you do today is important because you*
> *are exchanging a day of your life for it.*
> *When tomorrow comes, this day*
> *will be gone forever.*
> *In its place is something that you have left behind.*
> *Let it be something good."*
> *-Unknown*

Wow, what an incredible quote! The comment that grabs me the most is, "What you do today is important because you are trading a day of your life for it." The only thing to me worth trading a day of my life for, is something I love.

By deciding to become proactive with something you love, you will see that there are hundreds of jobs out there that will allow you to live the life so many long and wish for; a career where you actually get paid to do something you love, a job that you will actually look forward to going to! Maybe you're still a little confused because, like so many, you had the misconception that a career was supposed to be boring and like a ball and chain that ties you down.

Job 101
Let's say growing up, you wanted to play a professional sport but didn't have the natural physical talent to make it in the world of professional sports. Does this mean you have to give up your lifelong dream of having a career in professional sports? Of course not! Why not go into coaching or colour commentary, where you would actually be getting paid to call the games of your favourite team? There are so many other opportunities, from talent scout to GM or even sports therapy. Becoming proactive with what you love actually allows you to get paid for what you love to do and there is no greater job satisfaction than that.

> *"When you are just interested in something, you do it only when it's convenient; when you are committed, you accept only results, not excuses."*
> -Dr. Kenneth Blanchard

Does this just apply to sports? Of course not! This applies to everything that is life; if you love horses, go into a field that involves horses. If you love music, go out and get involved in the music industry. Both P-Diddy and Kanye West dropped out of college to pursue what they loved. Do you get what I am saying here? What good is a job that you hate? You are going to spend more than 90,000 hours working in your life, so you better enjoy what you do. Tony Hawk didn't skateboard because he knew he was going to become a millionaire. He skated because he loved it. Do what you love and the money will follow.

> *"Where the spirit does not work with the hand, there is no art."*
> - Leonardo Da Vinci

Decide to become proactive with what you love and you will never work a day in your life. For some reason, when choosing a career, most people don't do what they love, but rather what they think is going to make them rich. Once we eliminate money as our number one objective in a career, we begin to see a much clearer portrait of what the world holds for us.

Why is it that we are willing to spend so much time on the things we hate and so little time on the things we love? It just doesn't make sense to me. Life is too short to not be enjoyed. We, especially in North America, have been given so many opportunities to living a great and rewarding life. Why not take full advantage of it? Be the thing in life that you are most proud of.

There are only so many tomorrows before opportunity slips away. Become proactive with what you love so you can tell your son or daughter, "I don't know why they call it work. They should have called it fun!"

This is so important to remember: if it's your dream, it's probably someone else's too. So what are you doing to make sure you are the one who gets it? How hard are you willing to push yourself to accomplishing greatness? Simply wishing for it isn't enough.

Too Many Choices
I recently had a conversation with a close friend of mine about what career path she was going to follow. I explained to her my theory on becoming proactive with what you love. She then explained to me that while she agreed with my theory, she loved so many things and couldn't possibly decide on one single field to focus. This has become the ironic reality that our generation must now face. Our society has advanced so much that when it comes to picking a career from the diverse pool of job opportunities, we actually have too many options! We have so many options, in fact, that it has almost become impossible to decide which great opportunity to take.

So How Do We Cope?
It's really quite simple: Inside your heart lies the truth about you. Inside your heart lies what you already know. I truly believe if you look inside your heart and ask yourself this one honest question, you will find the answer. The question is, "What can I not imagine being a part of my life?" For myself, it was writing. For others, it may be something completely different. What do you truly love to do?

Stepping out and risking it all for some little voice that you hear inside your head is absolutely the most terrifying thing that you can do. It is also, without a doubt, the most rewarding thing you can do in life. I have watched as others go to school for something that they are only slightly interested in, and in return, they receive only slight satisfaction. Do what you love, and in return, you will receive true satisfaction. In life, you can decide to be good at a lot of things, or you can choose to be truly great at only a few. I don't know how you feel about your life, but I would much rather be great or the best at one thing, than be average at a lot of things.

Do whatever it is you have to do!
If you have to go back to school, swallow your pride and go. I cannot say this enough. **Swallow your pride**. Remember, to climb any size mountain, you must start from the absolute bottom.

Make the decision that you will work as hard as you have to, in order to get whatever it is you want out of life. Do what you have to, do to get what you want to get! I will share something very personal with you: I do not have strong English skills. In fact, it takes me twice as long to write a proper paragraph as a normal person my age. I'm also a pathetic speller and probably spelled every word written in this book wrong. (Thank God for spell check.) Given this information, you can only imagine how hard I had to work to write this book. I had to go back to school to upgrade my English skills. I had to swallow my pride. I had to stay in on nights when everyone else was out partying to read, learn, and create not only this book, but also my own domino effect. To achieve greatness, you must learn to sacrifice and do whatever is necessary to accomplish your dream. Personally,

I have realized that I don't want to be eighty and on my deathbed saying, "I really wish I would have tried to write a book." I don't want to live a life of regret. There is no promise anyone will ever read these words I have written. I am simply being proactive with what I love and will gladly trade a day of my life to do it. Don't allow pride to be a wall keeping you from true success and happiness.

"The difference between winners and losers is winners are willing to do things losers aren't."
- Dr. Phil

The above quote by Dr. Phil is something you truly need to remember. Every time you feel like giving up, or whenever you feel pride tugging at you, remember that quote. I'm telling you, the feeling of living a dream and accomplishing your goals is better than sex, alcohol, or drugs. Trust me, I have had all of them and it doesn't even compare. This is your fight. This is your battle.

"How much do you truly know about yourself unless you have been in a fight?"
- Brad Pitt (Fight Club)

The decision is yours: Begin taking the steps toward accomplishing your goals, or live a life full of questions about what could have been. My fourth grade principal, Mr. T, presented me with ten little words that have never left my side:

"If it is to be, it is up to me."

Dawn's Back up First Plan
I want to make something very clear and it's a decision that you need to be completely honest and open with yourself about. I have listened to way too many people who talk about going to school as a back up plan to whatever it is they actually wish they could be doing. I will give you an example: Dawn is a very good singer. True, she's no Alicia Keys, but she is a good singer. Dawn's true passion in life is

singing. From the time she wakes up until the time she goes to bed, all Dawn thinks about is how great it would be to become a singer. While trying to figure out what she wants to do with her life, Dawn decided that she should have a backup plan in case she never makes it as a singer. She has decided to go to college in the fall to study business. To many people, this may sound like a completely good idea. This, however, is why Dawn will never live her dream. It is completely true that school is never a bad idea and education is one of the most important things in the world. With that being said, there is a whole other world of education that comes outside of a school setting. It may sound like Dawn is on her way to creating her own positive domino effect. However, if Dawn truly, more than anything, wants to be a singer, then the classroom is the last place she should be (unless, of course, it is a music classroom). Dawn's backup plan has now become her main focus. If you're going to school, it is hard enough to keep up good grades with a part-time job, never mind while trying to chase after another dream. When you're in school, it should be your main interest. The ten thousand dollars she has decided to spend this year in school is now ten thousand invested in a backup plan. So what has she invested in the original plan? Singing to the mirror, or in the shower is fun, but it's not going to get you a recording deal. Dawn should have spent the ten thousand on singing lessons and hiring an agent that would get her in all the venues she needs to be in to get noticed. She should spend that ten thousand on her demo and not on a diploma, something she never intends to use anyway. By spending all her time and money on a backup plan, she never actually lives her first plan. Before she even starts, she has admitted defeat to her true dream.

Why? Because she is overcome with fear and the lack of self-belief that she can actually make it in the recording world. It is an all-too-real truth that many people do not believe in themselves enough to chase after a burning desire.

Back to Dawn's Pipe Dream
If you're going to make it and be the best at something, it has to be your whole focus and not just a pipe dream in the back of your head.

The program Dawn has entered is just another ball and chain holding her back from her true love, which is singing. Even if Dawn graduates with a degree in business, do you think she is actually going to use it? More importantly, will she ever really be satisfied with a life that does not involve her true passion?

She is more likely to bounce around from job to job, wishing she could find a job that brings her fulfillment, when all she had to do was sing in the first place. I think I should make it very clear what I'm saying here. **DO NOT** drop out of school because you think this book just told you to. **DO NOT** quit your job because you think this book just told you to. What I have just talked about is not for everyone. Many of you will try, and many of you will fail, especially if you are only doing it for the fame. Dawn may only make twenty thousand dollars a year being a singer. She may only sing weddings and bar mitzvahs. Dawn probably won't be the next Britney Spears. What Dawn has done, though, is followed her heart. She is getting paid to do what she loves and there is no greater job than that.

> *"The secret of success is making your vocation your vacation."*
> *- Mark Twain*

There are singers you will never hear from who have one hundred times the talent of Britney Spears, yet these singers will never get the fame or recognition that Britney has received. Investing in your dream life instead of a backup plan is not an option for everyone. I strongly recommend that only the people who are truly committed to going after their dreams think about this option. I only recommend this to the person who will risk it all in the name of love for what they're doing.

If you're not going to chase after your dream, then find a new one worth chasing. You must, however, let go of the old one because it will eat away at you for the rest of your life. You will likely find yourself saying to yourself, "I wonder what would have happened if I..." I'm currently chasing my own dream life... not for money, not for fame. I'm completely in love with every word written in this book. From the biggest word to the period that ends this sentence. I'm in love with what I do. I don't want to do anything else. Unless you are that committed, don't put it all on the line, because you will never make it. So I guess the question you have to ask yourself is, "Is it worth the risk to me?"

Don't feel bad if you say no; it's not for everybody.

Many tightrope walkers walk with a safety net, believing that it will protect them should they fall. Others walk without the net, believing that it does nothing but allow them to fall. So you have to ask yourself: Are you someone who walks the tightrope of life with a safety net, or are you the type to allow nothing but the other side of the rope to be your final outcome. The choice is yours... make sure you choose wisely.

> *"Fear not that thy life shall come to an end, but rather fear that it shall never have a beginning"*
> *-John Henry Cardinal Newman*

There is nothing more painful than watching your dreams fade away, right before your eyes.

I want you to try stepping out of your box of comfort and into a world you have never been before. There is much to see and learn with little time to do it. What are you waiting for? Turn your dreams into reality!

It Is Not a Game
I have read the same analogy over and over again, that life is a game. This is the most reckless way anyone could possibly describe the time we have on earth. Life isn't a game. Life is life. When a game is over, you can always choose to play it again. When life is over, it's over. We have to become much more aware of what's going on. It's time to awaken from your daydreams and realize that if you don't start making the decisions to create the results you want in life, then

you will have dreamed well but lived poorly! I am a human being, a creation of God, just as you are as well. We are entitled to all the happiness and success that the world has to offer. Make the decision to live life fully.

Keynotes to Remember for Chapter 2

- Every decision you make creates an action, which creates a result with your life.

- There is no wrong decision in life as long as you learn the lesson that comes along with it.

- Decisions involve commitment. Thoughts involve nothing.

- Decide to become proactive with what you love.

- You will spend more than 90,000 hours working in your life, so you had better love what you do.

- Don't allow pride to be a wall that stands in your way for success.

- Decide to turn your dreams into a reality.

Quotes to remember

"If it is to be, it is up to me."
- Mr. T. (not of the A-TEAM)

"The difference between winners and losers is winners are willing to do things losers aren't."
- Dr Phil

Workshop 2
It all starts with a decision!

Workshop Number 2

Action 1

Decide what *you* want. It's really that simple: Grab your notebook and write down everything you want out of life, whether it's a job, possessions, or relationships, write it all down.

Action 2

Make the decision to take action right now.

If you're unsatisfied with anything in your life, decide to take action right now and change it. Make the decision today that you're going to create momentum with your own personal domino effect by taking action. Remember, decisions create action and action creates results. So the only way to get a result is through making a decision.

Action 3

I want you to write down five or more decisions right now that you have been repeatedly putting off. Then, I want you to make up your mind and make the decision. Stick to your guns, whatever you decide on. Right now is the time to make your final decision. Don't bounce back and forth like a tennis ball. Once you have made the decision, it is done. Now be prepared for the consequences that will follow. It's funny looking back on all the "wrong" decisions I have made, because without them, I would have never written this book, and I would have never found my life's purpose. Make the decisions you have been putting off and just stick with them. Taking the next big step in your life is only a decision away.

> *"It is in your moment of decision
> that your destiny is shaped."*
> -Anthony Robbins

Self-reflection 1

> *"Every decision you make indicates
> what you believe you are worth."*
> - A Course in Miracles

This quote has forced me to do a lot of soul searching. I want you to really stop and think about the decisions that you have been making or have made in the past. What do they say about your own self-worth, and more importantly, what do you believe your worth is? If you believe that you are worth more than what you are living, begin to makes decisions that reflect it.

Question 1

When it comes to your life decisions, a question you need to ask yourself is, are you making these decisions for yourself? Or, are you making them for someone else? A perfect example of this is the story of Bill and his father, from Chapter 1. If you're a little confused, go back and reread the story. The worst thing that I could ever think of is waking up one morning and realizing that I am living someone else's dream. Remember, trying to please everyone but yourself will never lead to anything but failure.

> *"You are either living the life you have
> always dreamed of, or you are not."*
> - Jeffrey Moore

Remember that quote, because it is the absolute truth. Twenty years from now, when you're sitting back and reflecting on your life, *this* could be the moment you remember. The question is, how you will remember it? Will you remember it as the moment when it all changed…or will you remember it as the moment when you ignored that advice you should have taken?

Chapter 3
Television Dreams of Tomorrow

"There are those who do, and then there are those who watch television."
- Jeffrey Moore

Ahhhhh, television: the number one reason for procrastination and the place where I spent most of my adolescence. Aside from my mom and big brother, Craig McLennan, one of the biggest role models in my life was Zack Morris (which is really quite sad to admit).

Zack was the early 90s answer to the Fonz. Although he didn't have the jacket or bike, he made up for it with the world's biggest cell phone and his big- tongue Converses. Zack was the cool kid, both at school and at home. He was rebellious, good-looking, and able to get himself into (and out of) anything, no matter what it was. True, he had some pretty unrealistic talents, like being able to stop time, but he also had to deal with commercial breaks, so cut the kid a break!

So what happens when you idolize a fictional person? You begin to copy their actions, sayings, and dress. If Zack could pull off the stunts he did, I thought I could, too. Before I knew it, I was in trouble on a daily basis. I was pulling pranks and searching hard for my own Kelly Kapowsky. I did such a good job that my friend, Jamie McGrath, actually signed my yearbook, "Jeff, you're the closest I'll ever come to meeting Zack Morris."

In retrospect, I now know that instead of developing into my own person and creating my own attributes, I just stole his. In many ways, that is just what television has done. It has created armies of individuals who are all molded from the same original character. Think about it. After American Pie came out, how many Stiflers seemed to just pop up out of nowhere? Television has robbed our society of individualism and in its place left a big empty hole. I guess the question you have to ask yourself is, are you living your life or are you living vicariously through some TV character you can relate to? Are you your own identity or are you a created one? Life is great, especially when you live one.

TV Girl

Lisa is a college graduate who loves Louis Vuitton bags and everything else expensive. Her favorite show is Newlyweds because she dreams of one day living the life Jessica and Nick share together. She maxes out all of her credit cards trying to keep up with Jessica Simpson's amazing closet and life. When she's at work, she spends most of her day dreaming about her fake life. She has really started packing on the pounds from sitting in front of the TV, but she just can't find the time in her busy day to go to the gym. Her boss has just offered her some overtime and an opportunity for a raise, if she's willing to really put in some time. But it's five o'clock and the thought of missing out on one of her favorite celebrity shows is way too much to ask. Plus, tonight is the season finale of The OC and she needs to be well rested so she can truly enjoy the show! When she gets home, she throws her Louis Vuitton bag on her kitchen table, which is covered in overdue bills and gossip magazines. From the time she gets home until whenever she goes to bed, she sits on the couch eating junk and dreaming of a fake life. She spends a lot of time wondering why she is gaining so much weight, and why she can't afford to pay her credit card bills. Does this sound like anyone you know?

I can't even imagine the number of days I have wasted with completely good intentions to getting a lot done which somehow seems to turn into quality time with my favorite TV shows. Really think about how many times TV has been that sand trap in your life. Every time you try to pull yourself away, it pulls you in further until you can't move. Do an honest study with yourself. Write down how much time you waste in front of the television. Get creative and make a time sheet where you can track how much time you spend watching television. At the end of the week, you will have a pretty good idea of where your days, weeks, and years have gone. There are 168 hours in a week, so if you sleep eight hours a night, and work a total of forty hours a week, that still leaves you with seventy-two hours of the week that you are not utilizing. If you spent even half of the seventy-two hours in the week working on bettering yourself and getting what needs to be done finished, you would get so much further in life...further than you ever imagined possible.

I'm going to make it very clear that television, like most things, is okay in moderation, so pick a couple of shows you really enjoy and watch only these shows. Who are you really cheating by watching a rerun of That 70s Show that you have already seen a hundred times? We, as a society, have become so addicted to television that we are actually buying exercise equipment that is made so you can use it while watching TV!

Reality Love
Love is the number one thing sold and dealt with in all forms of entertainment. So what have we learned from years of corporate love brainwashing? Well, did you know you could fall head-over-heels in love with someone in just two commercial breaks? It's amazing! I hate to be the Scrooge on reality TV love, but BAH HUMBUG! If people weren't so bombarded with the so-called love they see on television, they wouldn't feel so desperate to find it in their own lives or feel like there is something wrong with them because they don't have it. People have actually gone love-hunting crazy. From the Internet to the work place, there is nowhere that humans are not actively trying to search for make-believe love. It's not real. You don't have it because it doesn't exist. Commercial products are the big winners when it comes to our fear of not finding television love. Everything, from zit cream to barbecue sauce and anything in

between, seems to tell us the same message; that if you don't meet the certain criteria that their product provides, then you will never find the love that you so badly want.

Everyone wants to kiss like they do on The Bachelor, but take a closer look and you will see that once the show ends, the couples never last.

Why don't they last? Because the people going on these shows have completely hidden agendas. They're not there for love; they're there to try to have fifteen minutes of fame or to possibly hook up with a rich member of the opposite sex, who will take care of their lazy ass. When the lights and cameras disappear, along with the huge house, carefree life, and amazing trips, it's time for a walk down Reality Lane. Suddenly they're greeted with the realization that without makeup and a professional hair stylist, their partner is not so attractive, and the fantasy starts to fade. Television is fake. Yeah, I said it. It's not real! Let me repeat that so it's very clear. Television is FAKE. Reality shows are FAKE. Game shows are FAKE. Everything is FAKE! So, if you do, and I suspect many of us do, please stop using it as a measuring bar for your own personal life. The sooner we realize that these people are just forms of entertainment and as real as a three-dollar bill, the sooner we will be able to let go of our unrealistic fantasies about how life should be. Don't beat yourself up because you haven't met your "Bachelor." True love does exist; it's just not on TV. True love is a couple that has been married for twenty-five years and still knows the meaning of unconditional love and the important lesson of forgiveness. It's not someone who entered a game show, had a couple of dates and is now, magically, ready for marriage. In four years, these so-called reality stars are going to be trying to get a job at Wal-Mart because no one else is going to take them seriously. Imagine if on every job interview you went to, the interviewer across from you said, "Hey, weren't you the big liar and cheater from Survivor?" or, "Hey, didn't you have sex with the Bachelor on your overnight date? He chose the other girl, right?"

Wow, sounds like a great life.

My Love Story
I was in love once, but by the time I realized it, she was gone. It hurt more than you can imagine being apart from her. I sat on my windowsill and tried not to cry as the rain fell. I requested our song on the radio hoping she would hear it and call me.

Wait a minute — that was an episode of Friends! Do you see what they have done? They have actually replaced my own memories with theirs. Damn you, TV!

Responsibility
This goes out to the movie stars and MTV celebrities, a.k.a. rap stars, pop stars, and especially, professional reality idiots (you know who you are): Every time you open your mouth, you are speaking to millions of young and impressionable youths. Whether you like it or not, you are role models. It comes with the job. So, please try to talk about something more important than how "fly" you are, how much money you make, or how big your house is. Just because you call out the city you were raised in does not mean you are representing your "hood". If you want to represent, go back to your community and buy some computers for the kids. Help rebuild some of our worn-down schools, instead of splurging on your fifth or sixth Mercedes. I don't want to hear about how you're "still the same" while your personal hair and makeup person touches you up. If you're still the same person, and you know where you're from, go back and help out the community, so others will not have to struggle as hard as you did.

Fourteen and Impressionable
The people I feel the most sorry for are the youth of today. They have become the innocent pawns of a major ratings war between television stations. The shock value in television has been upped in hopes of increased viewer ship.

After watching a recent reality show (which will remain nameless), I realized that television's social conscience has been thrown out the window. This reality show was the most offensive makeover show in history. If you're unfamiliar with it, the show I'm talking about takes ordinary women and gives them a complete makeover. Everything from lip and boob jobs, to liposuction, chin and butt implants - these women get the works! The idea is to change these "ugly ducklings" and turn them into something beautiful. I couldn't help but wonder how the average fourteen-year-old girl watching this show must feel. Any and all insecurities about herself have been exponentially magnified. Soon, instead of little girls wanting new clothes, they're going to ask their parents for a chin or cheek implant.

I can picture these girls looking in the mirror, hating what they see, and wanting to change so that they, too, can feel beautiful. The age of patients struggling with bulimia and anorexia seems to be at an all-time low. Hmmm, I wonder why! I don't have all the answers when it comes to youth and television. I'm not holding television solely responsible, but I am smart enough to know that it does play a major role. Anybody who says it doesn't is being completely ignorant to what is happening every day in this world.

Free Speech
There is always a lot of talk about free speech and I'm a huge supporter of it, especially when it's about art. I feel this book is a form of art and I would never want someone to tell me I couldn't write this book because of its extremely biased views. I'm sure that maybe even some would say that television shows are a form of art. So, I will never say you shouldn't watch TV, but what I will say is, let's not be slaves to the remote and empty promises which TV throws at us. Why don't we, as a generation, try to be the first since the invention of television to not bleedtelevision? To you young parents out there, let's try to spend more time playing and reading to the kids. Let's help them to grow their imagination instead of putting it to sleep. Growing up, my favorite memories weren't TV shows; they were playing board games with the whole family, which I still do to this day! Let's start spending more time doing what you're doing right now: reading.

Passing Thought
My passing thought for this chapter is that our generation has sold itself out. It has occurred to me that many people would rather vote for someone on American Idol than vote for the person who will run our country. If you don't vote when it really matters, then you don't have the right to complain about anything…especially your taxes or student fees.

So please put down the remote and see what is really going on out there.

Keynotes to remember For Chapter 3

- Television is fake.

- Television is fake.

- Television is fake.

- Television is fake.

- Television is fake.

- Television puts your mind to sleep.

Quote to Remember

"There are those who do, and then there are those who watch television."
- Jeffrey Moore

Workshop 3
Television; Lies for Tomorrow...

Workshop 3

Today's workshop is just a couple of simple exercises. The true aim of this workshop is to simply point out that while you sit there overindulging in television, the real world is passing you by. Second-by-second, moment-by-moment, and opportunity-by-opportunity!

Exercise 1
I want you to track how much time you spend in front of the TV during the week. A good way to do this is to create a time card, as I suggested earlier in the chapter. Track yourself for a week and then add up your hours. It may surprise you to see how much time you are actually spending in front of the TV. The only action television involves is wasted time.

Question 1
What has television added to your life? What has it given back to you that you could simply not do without?

Question 2
How has television taken away from your life? What else could you have been doing with all of that extra time? The people who often complain the most about there never being enough time in the day are usually the ones sitting in front of the television, procrastinating. Thirty years from now, are you going to be saying to yourself, "I am really glad I saw every episode of Desperate Housewives," or are you

going to be saying, "I am really proud of the actions I took towards reaching the life I have always dreamed of."

Question 3
When it comes to your life, are you using an unfair measuring stick, for not only yourself, but for others, as well? I know we would all love to date someone who looks like Jennifer Aniston or Brad Pitt, but the truth is, these models of perfection are completely unrealistic. Take time to look beyond some of the small flaws you see in the people around you and discover the real them.

Chapter 4
The Devil hiding out in your wallet...

"There are people who have money, and people who are rich."
-Coco Chanel

Have you ever really stopped to think about why we go green with envy? Hint: It is not because we're seasick. The Devil does exist, my friends! He has just changed his colour from red to green.

Money = Fear
Many of us, myself included, live in fear of not being money successful. Notice that I said "money successful" and not "life successful." There is a difference.

Why are we so willing to sell our souls to, as Cypress Hill said, "live large in the big house with five cars"? Why do we need to be seen driving a BMW or have that watch from Jacob the Jeweler? Why do we define who we are as a person by the type of "bling" we have? Why is it that we are so starved to look rich that we actually force ourselves to be completely broke? So many questions, but I believe there is one simple answer.

I think we do all these things just so we can show the people around us that we, too, are living the good life, when all we're really doing is living a lie! Stop for a second. Look at yourself and the person you are comparing yourself to. Realize you can never beat them and they can never beat you.

The Real Winners
Credit card companies, car dealerships, and banks are making a fortune off of the interest they charge us in our search to hide our insecurities with materialistic possessions. We need to stop forcing ourselves into financial woes before we end up in another major recession. We, as a generation, may actually bankrupt our whole country. Stop burying yourself in debt to make yourself look rich. I don't want to sound as if I'm preaching, because if I were, then I would be a complete hypocrite as I also struggle with the pursuit of celebrity wealth. I, just like many others, have an extreme fetish for expensive things. My favourite place in the world to shop is Lacoste. At eighty bucks for a cotton T-shirt, it can get very pricey, to say the least. (P.S.: I'm always on the lookout for sponsors. Hey, it's worth a shot!)

Lottery Dreams
The lottery: one of man's greatest gifts to man. I say that with complete sarcasm because, believe me, this is no gift of God. Gandhi has said that wealth without work can destroy you. This is why the lottery, that so many dream and long to win, is so incredibly dangerous. Imagine how your life would change if you won the lottery! Suddenly everyone you've ever been friends with feels like you owe them a piece of your money pie and before you know it, you feel like you are always second guessing people's intentions to be your friend. Life gets very complicated when money is involved.

Chris's Story
Chris is a broke twenty-three-year-old college dropout. Chris currently lives in a one-bedroom shack with no heat. This is very embarrassing for Chris and he tries to hide his own personal shame through plenty of daydreams, lies, and expensive clothes that he cannot afford.

It's a typical Friday for Chris. He spends most of his day socializing and trying to avoid doing any real work at his job. After work, Chris does his usual Friday routine of stopping off at the convenience store (where the cute blonde works), to pick up his usual Friday lotto ticket. As Chris exits the store, he is completely lost in his fantasies of what it would be like to win the lottery. Chris is so distracted that he does not see a homeless man lying on a subway vent in front of the store, trying to keep warm. Chris accidentally kicks the homeless man as he takes another step forward. The homeless man is startled and bites Chris on the leg. Chris resists the temptation to strike back at the homeless man, and instead, apologizes to him for being so clumsy. He feels a little embarrassed and offers to buy the homeless man a cup of coffee as a gesture. The homeless man accepts the offer and the two make their way over to a coffee shop. The homeless man thanks Chris for his generosity and hands him a gold coin. Chris looks at the gold coin and says, "I couldn't possibly accept this. The coffee was only a dollar and the coin seems to be worth much more than that."

The homeless man replies, "This coin is of no value to me anymore, for this is the gold coin of Aladdin. The coin will grant but one wish to its owner. Take it, but be very aware that with power comes great responsibility. I have used my one and only wish and ended up here. So please take this coin, but beware." Chris accepts the coin and then laughs to himself as he parts ways with the homeless man.

Chris then goes home and does his usual Friday night routine. As he undresses to get in the shower, the gold coin falls out of his pants pocket. Chris stares at the coin and then laughs out loud as he thinks, "Hey, it's worth a shot." He then grabs the coin and says, "I wish…that I win the ten million dollar jackpot tonight." Chris then jumps in the shower before going out with the boys. When Chris awakens in the morning, he gets the paper and does his usual routine of reading the comics and then sports before, of course, checking his lotto numbers. Chris pulls out his ticket and reads the numbers: 3-16-17-29-33-36. He then looks at his numbers and cannot believe that they match perfectly. Chris jumps for joy, screaming at the top of his lungs, "I'm rich…. I'm rich!" He then runs down to the lotto center and collects his earnings. Before he knows it, Chris is a local celebrity. He gets his picture on the cover of the local paper and wastes no time buying a beautiful home and a bunch of fast cars. Chris cannot believe his luck, as girls who never looked at him before are now glued to him. Even that cute girl at the convenience store has asked him out. Old high school buddies are calling him up to chill, and for the first time, life is starting to make sense for good old Chris. Finally, all of Chris's hard dreaming has paid off and he is living the life that he has always wanted.

However, as time continues, so too does his overspending.

Chris is beginning to notice he does not have as much money as he once had and his demands for luxury have only grown. Fast-forward ten years: Chris is sound asleep, when all of a sudden, he is awakened by some idiot who accidentally kicks him. Chris thinks that it is someone trying to steal his only blanket. He attacks the culprit by quickly biting him on the leg. The clumsy kid looks down and apologizes for his clumsiness, before offering to buy Chris a cup of coffee. I don't have to tell you where the story goes from here.

The Moral of the Story
Hey, I'm sure we would all love to win the lottery, but let's be honest: How many of us are truly ready for the responsibility of instant millions?

What is it that makes the lottery so appealing? The answer isn't probably what you would think. The true reason why most people dream about winning the lottery isn't the money. It's the chance to escape all of the poor decisions in life that they have made, but chosen not to change. The lottery is appealing because it's a quick fix with no work involved.

People want to win the lottery so they can escape their lives. They want to be able to erase all of their credit card debt, or quit the job they hate, but are stuck in. All of the mistakes and poor decisions they have made can be washed away with lottery money.

News flash: Most lottery winners go completely bankrupt within ten years. Why? Because they never change their decision patterns! A poor decision is a poor decision! No matter how rich you are, eventually all of your poor decisions will catch up with you. If you never appreciated money when you were poor, do you really think it's going to change when you become a lottery winner? I have said this before and I will probably say this again: You are a product of your own decisions. So, if you don't like who you are, begin changing your decisions today. Everybody has the ability to be rich and successful. Most people are just too lazy to accomplish it.

> *"Wealth is the product of a man's capacity to think."*
> *- Ayn Rand*

Hunters in Sheep's Clothing!

I've seen the credit card companies going to schools and basically giving away these cards for free. They like to lure people in by offering a free gift when you fill out the application form. It's almost like armed robbery. Credit card companies are like hunters. They place money under a box with a stick holding it up, and they tie a string to the stick, much like in the old Road Runner cartoons. When the unsuspecting prey (a.k.a. you) falls for the trap, they pull the string and trap you in.

> *"The problem is not how much we make...it's how much we spend."*
> *- David Bach*

Cast No Shadow

Look, I don't want it to make it sound like having the goal of being rich is a bad thing. It's definitely one of my goals, and I think it's something great to strive for. I just want you to remember that it's much harder to get rich by doing something you hate then it is to get rich by doing something you love.

Stay far away from "get rich quick" plans, because all they really are is "get much poorer and unhappier quick" plans. Aside from winning the lottery, it is simply not possible to become a millionaire overnight. There are, however, a million tiny steps you can take, day-by-day, to get there. Think about how much more rewarding it would be to become rich because you earned it as opposed to just stumbling across some lucky numbers.

So in your quest for financial freedom, make sure you love what you're doing and not trying to make yourself rich by chasing false hopes and promises.

Tim's Story of Envy
Tim is what you would call a money lover. He has no idea how, but he knows he is going to be rich. He's only twenty-one, and wonders why he doesn't already have three houses to his name. He was fortunate enough to grow up in an average-income family, but has always dreamed about a world full of bigger and better possessions. He listens to others around him talk about money and he drools at the thought of the life they speak of.

He takes note of what people say and has come up with a million and two "get rich quick" schemes. Everything from Internet porn, to door-to-door knife sales; you name it and he's tried it. But for some reason, every time he starts something, he quits before the ball ever really gets rolling. He gets extremely mad at himself for quitting and begins to believe he is somewhat of a failure.

He can never figure out why he can't just become a millionaire overnight. To Tim, and the many people who fall into the empty pursuit of money: The reason you are unsatisfied with your financial situation is because you're not doing what you love and you're chasing empty promises. In doing this, you are fighting a battle that you can't win. So be very honest with yourself: are you chasing after a dream, or are you chasing after money?

> *"Do what you love and the money will follow."*
> *- Marsha Sinetar*

If I were Britney, I would be rich
I know how frustrating life can be sometimes, especially when it feels like the world is on your shoulders, and you turn on your television and see Britney Spears or Justin Timberlake, who seem to have it so easy! It's so easy to become jealous of their superstardom, fame, and money. It's important to remember that Justin and Britney weren't just walking down the street when some guy grabbed them and said, "Hey, you're cute. Want to be a celebrity? Here, have forty million dollars too." These two were working harder at chasing their dreams, by the age of five, than most do in their whole lives. They were lucky enough to realize their dreams at very young age, and didn't spend all their time watching television or sleeping in every day. It didn't just happen over night.

Hard Work Is a Luxury
It's going to take a lot of hard work to get where you want to be. A very close friend of mine works two full-time jobs, about seventy hours a week. She never complains or gets mad about how much she works. The end result is she has paid off her student loans and is about to buy her first house, in less than three years after graduation (not too shabby, eh?). Hard work is the key to a successful life. I'm not saying working seventy hours a week is the only way to get ahead, but it's not a bad idea either.

Slow Down
Enjoy this amazing part of life you have now entered. Stop rushing through life at 500 miles an hour. Just because you're done with school, and for the first time ever, really starting to make some coin, it doesn't mean you should get married, have kids and start your boring adult life. The divorce rate stands at 50 percent. Why? Probably because most take the plunge into married life way too early and really can't afford it. I don't know about you, but I don't want to be paying alimony when I'm twenty-four.

You Only Get Ten Years
The ten years you get, from the ages of twenty to twenty-nine, are to build yourself up for your happy and successful thirties. I don't want

to be thirty, divorced, in debt, and stuck in some job I hate. Wake up! We're still growing up, not all grown up, so enjoy this time of freedom and personal growth that you have right now

Keynotes to Remember for Chapter 4

- The lottery is the lazy and unmotivated man's dream.

- Most lottery winners go bust.

- You are the product of your decisions, so if you don't like who you are, begin changing your decisions today.

- Don't fall victim to credit card companies.

- Follow your heart and what you love, and the money will come.

- You only get nine years to design your thirties, so slow down and enjoy this part of life.

Quote to Remember

"Wealth is the product of a man's capacity to think."
- Ayn Rand

Workshop 4
Money, cash, bling isn't everything.

Workshop 4

Question 1
Are you living a lie? Be very honest with yourself: are you living within your means or are you trying to portray an image? If you are portraying an image, allow me to introduce you to a word that is in you're near future: BANKRUPTCY.

Question 2
Do you control your spending habits, or do your spending habits control you?

Self Realization 1
We all go through periods in life where money can be extremely tight. Then somewhere along the way (maybe after working a few doubles or a nice tax return), we are reintroduced to the lovely feeling of having cash. The problem with money is that it makes us quickly forget what it was like to be poor and before we know it, we are over-spending and come back to the reality of being poor again. I remember when I was completely broke in college and whenever I was actually able to come across some money, the first thing I would do is spend it. Take time to really examine your spending habits, not only when you are poor, but also when you have some cash to play with.

Question 4
Have you started to track the hours you spend in front of your television? If not, I strongly suggest you start now.

Question 5
What decisions have you made over the last few days to truly start creating your own domino effect for success? Remember, every decision you make creates an action, so by deciding not to do anything, you are still creating an action, which in turn creates a domino effect.

Question 6
What one decision are you still avoiding or putting off that could drastically change your life? The longer we decide not to do something, the less time there is to do it!

Question 7
Have you figured out what it is you truly love to do yet?

Chapter 5
The Key to Success Is To Surround Yourself with It...

"Grand adventures await those who are willing to turn the corner."
- *Chinese fortune cookie*

Here is one of the important unwritten rules of life: You are what you surround yourself with. So, let's ask the question, "What are you surrounding yourself with?"

Look, I'm not going to beat around the bush on this one. If you surround yourself with drunks, you, in turn, will become a drunk. Sorry, but it's true. If you surround yourself with lazy, underachievers, you, in turn, will become an underachiever. Take a good look around you, especially at cliques. Why are the "skaters" called "skaters?" Hint... because they all skate. Why are the "jocks" the "jocks?" Or why are the "potheads" the "potheads?" If you are a person who has never smoked pot before, but have recently become best friends with a bunch of potheads, then I am willing to bet you're going to start smoking pot on a regular basis. It's not that difficult to get caught up in your surroundings and what you surround yourself with is a direct reflection of how society sees and treats you.

"Those who follow the crowd usually get lost in it."
-Rick Warren

Look, if you want to become a priest, but you surround yourself with pimps and hookers, then there is a pretty good chance no one will ever take you seriously.

If you're trying to elevate yourself beyond the stars, ditch the dead weight. It's hard enough to fly without wings; sometimes you have to say good-bye to the ones you love, the ones that you know are holding you back. You know who I am talking about.

I am talking about the ones who are not growing up and the ones that don't seem to have the same desire for success as you do. In the pursuit of fulfilling your dreams, you will need to make many major sacrifices. Some, unfortunately, will have to be people who choose to do nothing with their lives and in turn help to make sure you do nothing with yours. People are afraid of change. If you're surrounded by underachievers and you decide it's time to better yourself, I guarantee you will be faced with unforeseen challenges. You see, as you start to achieve success by creating a positive domino effect, some people will start to feel resentful because they aren't doing anything with their lives. It is these people that you need to watch out for because it is easier for them to try and bring you down than for them to become proactive with their own lives.

"No matter where you go, there you are."
- Buckaroo Banzai

Being You Means Being an Individual
Are you being an individual, or are you just another face in the crowd? Individualism is rare and something that is so needed today. The most important thing in life is to be true to yourself. This will seem like a very easy thing to do, but in reality it is a true battle. Stepping out of a crowd and announcing you are who you are takes much courage. Many around you will feel alienated and threatened

by your boldness. Don't allow other people to distract you from following the path of life you want to walk.

Follow your heart and be your own individual.

> *"Keep away from people who try to belittle your ambitions. Small people always do that, but the really great make you feel that you, too, can become great."*
> *- Mark Twain*

Poison Kills Individualism

Poisonous people have a habit of trying to kill individualism. We all know many poisonous people. They are everywhere in life. They are the ones who are always quick to point out why you will fail. Poisonous people are a cancerous plague, which if allowed, can deflate anyone's courage to strive for the best.

So how can you tell if you have poisonous people around you?

They are not hard to spot. They come in all forms: parents, girlfriends/boyfriends, best friends, co-workers, teachers, and just about any other aspect of your life where you communicate with someone on a regular basis. The way to really catch or spot one is to throw out an idea. Throw out something like, "You know, I think I will write a book" or, "I think I will go to school to study fashion." Choose something that is ambitious but not completely out of left field. Telling someone you want to be a professional camel breeder may bring out negative thoughts from anyone, no matter how positive a person they are. (However, if your heart is in it and you really want to become a camel breeder, I bet there is big money in it. If you act now, you could corner the North American market! You never know, camels could become the next potbelly pig, so good luck with it).

> *"To be independent of public opinion*
> *is the first formal condition*
> *of achieving anything great."*
> - George Wilhelm Hegel

Poisonous people love to point out every little reason they believe you will fail. Here are some of the more common excuses used by poisonous people…

"It will never work."

"You're too young/too old."

"No one wants a camel."

> *"I don't know the key to success, but the key*
> *to failure is trying to please everybody."*
> - Bill Cosby

Life can be incredibly difficult if you have poisonous parents. You must learn to believe in the strength of yourself. Find positive people to share your ideas with. Constructive criticism is always needed, but it should never be the only direction the conversation goes. Something else that's very important to realize is that the world is full of poisonous people. Maybe you are a poisonous person. Take a good look at yourself. Are you someone who always looks for the negative in any situation? If you are a poisonous person, then you probably suffer from the fear of others being more successful in life than you. Step out of your old shadows and fears, and into a new light.

> *"Great spirits have always encountered*
> *violent opposition from mediocre minds."*
> - Albert Einstein

Poison Love

I especially want to warn you about poisonous boyfriends/girlfriends. Sometimes in the overpowering fog that love and lust can create, we are completely blind to seeing what our significant other really does to us. I have observed this firsthand, as a very close friend of mine was completely caught up in an incredibly physically and mentally abusive relationship. If the person you are with abuses you, either physically or mentally, you need to rid yourself of them immediately. The longer the cycle continues, the harder it is to escape. If your close friends are warning you about the person you are seeing, take a closer look. For some reason, many people choose to stay with partners who do not respect them and who do not treat them as equals. The first step to a successful relationship is to respect each other. Don't allow someone to run your life and treat you one ounce less than you expect to be treated. You are a human being and deserve to be treated as one. Don't ever confuse the feeling of comfort and routine with love and happiness. THEY ARE NOT THE SAME.

For some strange reason, it seems that humans want to protect their abuser. Stop it! The feeling of love may actually be a feeling of fear for your own safety. Abuse can leave you feeling like you don't deserve any better, when the truth is, you deserve so much more. Don't settle for one ounce less.

The fear that abuse brings into a person's life is very powerful. I have seen many people with such great potential sell themselves short by choosing to continue these poisonous relationships. I am issuing a personal challenge to escape the cancer that poisonous people bring into our lives. If you are in an abusive relationship, please escape it...NOW.

It's time for some brand-new thinking for some old-time problems and perspectives.

> *"Poor is the man whose pleasures depend
> on the permission of another."*
> -Madonna

Saying Goodbye Is Sometimes the First Step to Success

Growing up, there is no harder decision than choosing to separate yourself from close friends who only serve to bring you down. I have said goodbye to many of mine. Growing up, we were like brothers. I find it extremely hard to watch as many of my good friends slip away into what they are becoming. Many have fallen into hard drugs. Many continue to abuse alcohol. Many are going nowhere yet do absolutely nothing about it. Trust me, I fully understand how hard it is to say goodbye or distance yourself from people you love. What you must realize is that you only get so many chances at success. You only get so many chances to become something special. You have to understand that it is time to grow up and it is time to stop giving in to peer pressure to self-destruct.

What you really have to ask yourself is, "What are the people who I choose to surround myself with doing with their lives?" If they are doing excessive amounts of drugs or not trying to move forward, then there is a very good chance they will begin to pull you down with them. I know I am the only person responsible for my ultimate destiny. I won't allow anyone to stand in my way or try to bring me down. Why should you? If I have to walk alone to be successful, then I am just happy to be walking.

Brad's Story

In life, we create self-identities that we are constantly selling to ourselves and others. The following is a story of how one person's desire to fit in created a negative domino effect. Brad is a twenty-one-year-old kid who went from being a nobody to being a somebody through the magic of cocaine. Brad is a smart kid, however he continues to make dumb decisions. Brad's desire to fit in with an older crowd led him to experiment with cocaine. While he gets a rush from the drug, Brad is really high on his newfound popularity. Showing up at parties with the drug has made him more friends than he could have ever imagined. Loving the feeling of acceptance, Brad begins doing coke on a more-than-regular basis. One year flies by, and Brad has now acquired a pretty serious drug problem. Luckily for Brad, he lives at home and doesn't pay rent, so all of his hard-earned money can go to his addiction and he doesn't have to worry about becoming homeless…yet. Brad feels like the quality of his life is declining and he has noticed a growing dependence on cocaine to be able to function properly. What Brad doesn't realize is that it isn't his dependency for coke that led him into this situation. You see, Brad has thought about quitting many times. However, the thought of not having a drug problem is not as important to Brad as his cokehead friends. Brad worries that if he gives up drugs, he won't be accepted into this crowd anymore. Brad's dependency to be someone in this crowd is more powerful and more important to Brad than getting clean. What a sad life Brad will have lived, when eventually all of his friends fade away and all he is left with is an addiction.

Why do so many aging twenty-something's choose to constantly abuse substances and not grow up? I'll tell you why. It is their search to still fit in and be a part of the crowd. High school is over, kids, and it's no longer about fitting in as much as it is about finding your way. Going out and getting crazy drunk four times a week isn't cool anymore. Going out and ripping some rails has never been cool. You are not impressing anyone by being able to snort the fattest rail in the group. I know change can be a difficult thing to face. When I faced the fact that I had to change, I was scared. It sounds stupid, but I thought that if I wasn't this "jerk" party guy who said the most vulgar and rude things and was sleeping with everything that moved, then I wouldn't be accepted or fit in anymore. I mean I wouldn't be "Jeff Moore" and if I wasn't "Jeff Moore" then, who was I? It was after I said those words that I realized I was never actually being myself in the first place. We all live and create these personas who we believe we are. I have realized that for me to be me, I must first really be me. I have become extremely bored with being this character I used to play.

Are you being who you really want to be? Or are you being who you think people expect you to be?

If you stand up for your life and begin to make a change for the better, there is no doubt in my mind that you will face opposition and challenges from friends. You see, humans fear change and more importantly, humans fear being left behind. There is a comfort in seeing you are not the only person with a problem. I remember one time, when I was working as a waiter and I was serving a table of four heavy-set women. One of the women at the table was talking about how she had lost five pounds on her new diet. The girls all listened and congratulated her with words of encouragement. I felt extremely guilty offering the dessert menu at the end of dinner but it's part of my job. When I offered the dessert menu, the three women who were not on a diet gladly accepted the dessert menus while the fourth said, "No, thank you. I am on a diet." Immediately, the other three women jumped all over her with reasons for why she should have dessert. Everything from "Look, they have your favorite," to, "I can't eat this by myself." I gladly took the menu back and left, hoping she would not give in. I was not surprised, however, when I returned and all four women ordered dessert. I remember looking into the eyes of the woman who was on the diet, as she ordered. I could see how disappointed she was in herself. That night, she broke her diet and I am willing to bet she never got back on track. It is my honest opinion that her friends really couldn't care less if she ate dessert or not that night. What they cared about was not being reminded of their own faults and seeing someone else improving their life as they continued to destroy theirs.

"If you don't run your life, someone else will."
- John Atkinson

I have already said this, but it's so important that I must say it again: You are what you surround yourself with. If you want to change, say goodbye to the people who choose not to or who do not support your positive domino effect.

Walking alone can be tough, but it is much easier than trying to fit in and change at the same time.

Keynotes to Remember For Chapter 5

- You are what you surround yourself with.

- What you surround yourself with is a direct reflection of who you are, whether it is fair or not.

- Poisonous people exist in all forms of your life.

- Life is not about trying to fit in as much as it is about finding your own path.

- It's important to be your own leader and to not follow others.

Quote to Remember
"You are what you surround yourself with."
                     - Jeffrey Moore

Workshop 5

Who are you, anyway?

Workshop for Day 5

This workshop is all about waking you up to the truths that you may be blind to seeing.

Self Reflection 1
I'm sure you have heard the old saying, "Sticks and stones may break my bones, but words will never hurt me." I'm going to tell you right now that nothing could be further from the truth. Words can hurt you and can kill any momentum you may have created in a personal domino effect for success.

I want you to take a moment, right now, and look at the people you choose to surround yourself with. Whose words seem to add to your life, and whose seem to take value away?

Self Reflection 2
In life, there will always be those who seek to lead and those who are much more content to follow.

When it comes to your life and the direction you seem to be headed, are you leading, or, are you following others? Are you actively searching for what you want out of life, or, are you just following those around you, who are taking you in a direction you may not want to be headed?

A perfect example of this once again was the story of Bill. If you have forgotten it go back to Chapter 1 and reread it.

Action 1
Take control of your life. Become your own leader. You are the most important person in your life! Stop standing on the sidelines and get active. Go out and ask questions. Make some decisions and get this domino effect started RIGHT NOW! Push yourself harder than you have ever had to push. Believe in yourself more than you ever thought was possible and take action in accomplishing things that need to be done in your life. Create the domino effect you so desire.

Chapter 6
That Other Four-Letter Word That Starts With F
F.E.A.R
False...Evidence...Appearing...Real

"Our deepest fear is not that we are inadequate.
Our deepest fear is that we are powerful
beyond measure. It is our light, not
our darkness, that frightens us.
We ask ourselves, who am I to be brilliant,
gorgeous, talented and fabulous?
Actually, who are we not to be?
You are a child of God.
Your playing small doesn't serve the world.
There's nothing enlightened about shrinking so
that other people won't feel insecure around you.
We are born to make manifest the
glory of God that is within us
It's not just in some of us, it's in everyone.
And as we let our light shine, we unconsciously
give other people permission to do the same.
As we are liberated from our own fears, our
presence automatically liberate others."
-source: A Return to Love by Marianne Williamson
(As quoted by Nelson Mandela in his inaugural speech, 1994)

If you're not living the life you want, I'm willing to bet fear is playing a major role in it. This four-letter word is the rock that can shatter anyone's window of hope.

A Fear Diagnosis

To give meaning to the word fear with one general definition is impossible, for fear is like Baskin Robbins: there are at least thirty-one different flavors. However, if I were going to define fear, I would diagnose it as a self-limiting belief or excuse for not attempting something in life. All too often, people live behind their fears and use them as excuses for why they are where they are in life. Some people fear hard work because their comfort zone is being lazy and sitting on the couch. Some people fear change because their comfort zone is their daily routine. Fear is usually something that takes us out of our comfort zone and into a new realm. When you step out of your comfort zone and into a new realm, you begin to grow and recreate who you are as a person, and when you recreate who you are as a person, you recreate what is possible in your life.

> *"Do the thing you fear, and the death of fear is certain."*
> *- Ralph Waldo Emerson*

My Heroes

On 9/11, hundreds of rescue workers rushed to the scene of the most tragic and unbelievable act of terrorism in American history. The courageous rescue workers showed no fear in rushing into two burning buildings to save the lives of complete strangers. This meant risking and losing many of their own lives in the process. Were these true heroes victims of fear? Absolutely not! So how did these ordinary men and women overcome some extraordinary fears?

I watched a firefighter being interviewed later that week on the evening news. The news reporter asked the firefighter if he was scared during his daring rescue attempts. His answer to the question was one that really sparked my interest as he stated, "You know what,

I really wasn't. I guess I just didn't have time to think about it. I just knew what had to be done." I found his answer to the question very fascinating. He didn't have time to think of fear, so he had no fear. That firefighter taught me a valuable lesson that day when it comes to facing your fears. The reason we so often become stricken with fear is because we sit there and think about it over and over again. What if I fail? What if I'm not good enough? What if it all comes crashing down on me? Your brain now has so many reasons to be scared of failing, you probably will. If you want a better answer, ask a better question. Instead of "What if I fail?" how about asking, "What if I succeed?"

If the courageous workers on 9/11 would have been told, "Hey, guys, just so you know, tomorrow two planes are going to crash into both World Trade towers. It will be the single largest terrorist attack on American soil to date. People will be plummeting to their deaths all around you. Your lives, and the lives of everyone around you, will be at risk. Oh, and before I forget, about an hour or so after you show up, both Trade towers will collapse, trapping many of you inside. Take a good look at the person sitting next to you, because it may be the last time you see them. Enjoy spending what could be your last meal with your wife and kids and I'll see you tomorrow…"

If all of the rescue workers had been provided with that information before 9/11, how do you think they would have handled it? I'm not trying to take anything away from any of the courageous heroes of 9/11, I'm simply just trying to put things into perspective.

"Courage is not the absence of fear, but rather, the judgment that there is something else more important than fear."
-Ambrose Redmoon

You Are Somebody
When dealing with your ultimate fears that come along in life, how do you respond to them? Do you confront them or do you allow your fears to win?

> *"People's fears are only as powerful as people make them."*
> —Marilyn Manson

The Cure for Fear
I, just like everyone else in this world, have had to battle many fears in my lifetime. Every time my brain gives me a reason to fear something, I think long and hard about what having this fear is going to cost me. Then I say to myself, "I am somebody and screw it: No fear is going to get in my way." When I wrote this book, I had to battle many fears. I had the fear that I was just wasting my time. I had the fear that people would read this book and laugh at my thoughts. Then I remembered that I am somebody and I will never allow a few stupid self-made fears to control my life. That's when I came up with this quote!

> *"I shall overcome any fear in my life that tries to rob me from my true potential and allows me to forget who I truly am as a person."*
> - Jeffrey Moore

I want you to feel the power of my quote. Grab that fear! It's the one that has been sitting on you, crushing you, and making you feel as if you were carrying an extra five hundred pounds of personal weight. I want you to take it by the neck and repeat my quote with a sense of strength and conviction. Look your fears in the eye and say these powerful words. You tell them, "I am somebody and I will no longer allow you to control my life."

Playing It Safe Is the Most Dangerous Way
For some reason, in life, many people get confused and actually believe that playing it safe is the best way. In reality, playing it safe is just the coward's way. All that playing it safe allows you to do is to live a life ruled by fears; a life that will, at best, be completely and utterly boring. What is there to gain from never taking any risks?

Life is a journey from the time we are born until our final moments. It's one giant highway, with endless exits and detours that can take us through many highs and lows. We must learn to appreciate both the highs and lows. They are the scenery and the still frames in our minds that help to remind us of what it was like at this particular part of the journey. The problem that so many face in life is a lack of real direction. All too often, people follow others, believing that they must know the way. The reason so many choose to always follow and never lead is because from the time of birth until death we are always being told what to do; first, by our parents, then, by our teachers, and finally, by our bosses. Humans have a natural fear when it comes to the unknown or change. Many people fear taking the leadership role with their lives because if they fail, there is no one to blame but themselves. Many people never take control of their lives because they don't think they know how. I think it's important to remember at one point in your life you didn't know how to read and now, look at you, you're close to completing this book! You're taking the steps you need to take in order to make the positive domino effect that will get you the life you deserve. Good for you!

Death Becomes Us
I recently went to a wake for a friend's family member. While I was at the funeral home, I couldn't help but think of the many times I had been there before, and the inevitable thought that one day, I too would have my final visit here. For some strange reason, I'm always thinking about my own death and particularly, my funeral. I think about who would attend and what would be said on my day of passing. In the book, The Seven Habits for Highly Effective People, by Steven Covey, there is an exercise in which you write three eulogies for your own funeral: one from a family member, another from a close friend, and finally one from a co-worker. Doing this exercise can be a very self-reflective and eye-opening experience. It really forces you to think about who you are, and what you want to become as a person.

What is fear except something that you have created? What do you truly want to be said about you when your time is called?

Do you want to hear that you challenged your fears and overcame any obstacle in your way to achieving your dreams? Do you want to hear that you lived a life of success? Or, would you rather hear that you never really did much but sleep and watch a lot of TV? I know that, personally, I want to be remembered for greatness and not mediocrity. The only way I can do this is to fight through my fears every day to accomplish what needs to be done.

Last Wake-up Call
The only thing that is certain in life is death, so stop fearing life! If today were your last, what fear would you wish you had conquered yesterday?

> *"Though I walk through the valley of the shadow of death, I will fear no evil."*
> *- Psalms 23:4*

Chapter 6 Keynotes to Remember

- Fear is a self-limiting belief.

- Stepping out of your comfort zone helps to recreate who you are, thus recreating what is possible in your life.

- Your fears are only as big and as real as you believe them to be.

- If you choose to follow instead of lead, you can't get mad when the person in front of you leads you to somewhere you don't want to be. Take the leadership role in your life; create your vision and find a way to getting there through overcoming your fears.

Quote to remember

"I shall overcome any fear in my life that tries to rob me from my true potential and allows me to forget who I truly am as a person."
- Jeffrey Moore

Workshop 6
Fear Busters

Workshop 6

Question 1
I want you to list the ways you usually allow fear to control your life. In other words, what self-limiting actions do you take that are fear-based? A perfect example is not trying snowboarding because you fear people will make fun of you if you aren't very good. Not trying because of fear of other people's reactions is a self-limiting action caused by fear that you allow to affect your life.

Question 2
List your five biggest fears when it comes to choosing a career or goal.

1.
2.
3.
4.
5.

After listing these fears, list what it will cost you if you don't overcome them, just like we did back in Chapter 1. Determine what these fears will cost you.

Action 1
I want you to write the quote below on a cue card. Every time you think of a fear that stops you from doing something, pull it out of

your pocket and read it to yourself. Overcoming your fears means taking control of your life and not allowing anything to stand in your way. This quote can really help to remind you who is in charge:

> *"I shall overcome any fear in my life that tries to rob me from my true potential and allows me to forget who I truly am as a person."*
> *-Jeffrey Moore*

Question 3
Name a past experience where you allowed a self-made fear to prevent you from accomplishing something. How did you feel after?

Question 4
What is one small action you can take today that would help to create a domino effect in overcoming one or all of your fears, and getting you that much closer to the life you want?

Question 5
What one major fear stands between you and the life you have always dreamed of? Once you have written it down, it is now time to confront it.

Question 6
what fear based decisions are you still putting off. Take this time right now to make the decision that you have feared making and take the next step in life.

Congratulations on making it this far. I'm willing to bet that more than 90 percent of the people who bought this book will never read these words. You should be very proud of yourself.

Chapter 7
Procrastination and Goals: Sitting on Both Sides of the Teeter-Totter

PROCRASTINATION: *To habitually put off doing something that should be done.*

When I say the word *procrastination* what do you think of? Do you envision yourself sitting in front of the television, feeling lazy and flipping through reruns? Or maybe you think of all the unnecessary naps that you take when you know you should be doing anything else. When I think of procrastination, I envision all of the many important things I should have done that I still haven't even started. I imagine all the unnecessary pain and frustration that comes along with procrastination. In fact, 90 percent of all the frustrations in my life are caused by unfinished business I have chosen to procrastinate over.

> *"The man who really wants to do something finds a way; the other man finds an excuse."*
> *- E. C. McKenzie*

Habits
Habits are the things we do on a daily basis that create who we are. The way we stand, eat, smile, and think, are all basically habits, and habits are nothing more than a learned behaviour.

We learn the majority of our habits from the people we spend the most amount of time with. This is why it is so common for children with parents who smoke, to pick up that nasty habit of smoking as they grow up. (Once again we are what we surround ourselves with.) The more we habitually see and practice a behaviour, the easier it becomes a part of our routine and thus, a habit. What may seem like absolute craziness to one person is merely a daily normality to someone else. For instance, someone who is habitually early would probably view the daily habits of someone who is habitually late as absolute craziness.

"Practice makes perfect," and the longer we practice the habits of our lives, the better we become at them, whether this is a good or bad thing.

When I stopped and took a close look at the things I was doing on a daily basis and becoming a master at, I figured out why I had ended up where I was and learned where my domino effect was taking me.

Good habits help to create success in our lives. They give us a great push in a positive domino effect and create a strong foundation to build on. Bad habits, however, are what force us into unrewarding lives. They are a giant push in the wrong direction. An easy way to begin success in your life is to stop and really take inventory of what habits you possess, both good and bad.

The Worst Habit of All
Procrastination is nothing more than just a bad habit: that's it. That being said, bad habits are what cause many with so much potential to fall short. So when I speak about habits, you must realize the word *habit* should never be taken lightly.

Very much like a smoker's habit to smoke, the procrastinator's habit of procrastinating can be very dangerous. Procrastination may seem like a very small and relatively harmless habit at first. But as the habit begins to grow, it soon turns into an out-of-control roller coaster that can take over your life. When I really forced myself to watch my procrastinating habits, I found many interesting ways I would procrastinate, without even knowing it. One of them was that I would clean my house, thus convincing myself that I was doing something positive. However, it wasn't what needed to be done. The lights will still turn on tomorrow, even if my house is a mess. They may not turn on, however, if I don't pay my electric bill.

Silly Boy
Oh, how I used to love to procrastinate (it's something I still battle to this day). I loved to just put things off until tomorrow, believing full-heartedly that I would then do whatever it was that needed to be done. However, we all know the old story: Tomorrow would come and go in a series of old *Jackass* and *Family Guy* reruns, and nothing would ever get done. As the days continued to pass, I seemed to get no closer to finishing what I needed to do. It was like digging a hole of personal sabotage, full of reruns and wasted moments. The only problem was that as I dug this imaginary hole, I forgot to allow myself a safe passageway out. Before I knew it, I had dug myself in so deep that I couldn't get out. I was completely stuck in this self-made hole, that in the beginning seemed so small and easy to escape.

Doesn't Make Much Sense
When it comes to procrastination, we all have our little habits we continually fall into. Procrastination really doesn't make a lot of sense to me. Why do we actually put off bettering our lives for needless boredom? Why do we decide something that needs to be done is less important than TV?

The Procrastinator's Myth
There seems to be a common myth that comes along with procrastination. I call it the Procrastinator's Myth. The myth is that, "It's okay to procrastinate because I work better under pressure." Do you know why it is that so many feel they actually work better under pressure? Is it because God has given them an amazing gift for this kind of situation? Probably not! The more likely answer is that for many people, they have procrastinated their whole lives and it is such

a constant habit that their brain has no idea of any other way to work, except under pressure.

Many choose to procrastinate in life because they are afraid of moving forward. Procrastination has a lot to do with trying to remain in our comfort zones. Procrastinating is the closest we can come to hitting the "pause button" in life. It is the closest we can come to trying to make the world stand still. However, the problem is that all of these wasted moments end up costing us more than we could ever imagine. The day when we decide to take our finger off the pause button and start working towards a life of fulfillment, we realize everything has passed us by. Just because we are in pause mode does not mean the world is. The only way to be taught the dangers of procrastination is to witness your dreams vanishing before your eyes.

Beating the Habit
So how do we beat this powerful habit that we have to face every day? How do we end, once and for all, the demons of procrastination?

First, like any other addiction or serious problem (and believe me it can be both), we must first admit that we have a problem. So, if you are a procrastinator (and I'm sure many of you are), stand up, look yourself in the mirror, and repeat after me: "Hi. My name is (fill in the blank) and I am a procrastaholic." Once you do this, it's time to rid yourself once and for all of this bad habit.

"An Hour a Day Helps to Keep Procrastination Away"
The reason so many people have such a hard time dealing with the habit of procrastination is because they have completely unrealistic ideas of how to stop. If you have been a serious procrastinator for the better part of your life, it is impossible to just quit cold turkey. I'm not a smoker, but after watching many of my friends try to quit smoking, and then watching myself try to quit procrastinating, I would compare them as very similar habits to kick. I would estimate that I have been a serious procrastinator for at least the last fourteen years of my life. Even in public school, I would procrastinate over doing something as small as a colouring assignment. This has led to a very strong habit

and a lot of wasted potential. I would say my level of procrastinating is comparable to a smoker who has been smoking at least a pack a day for fourteen years. A smoker of fourteen years, in most cases, does not just wake up one day and quit cold turkey. They're going to go through withdrawal symptoms and failed attempts, just like I did when dealing with procrastination. When I first started, I would tell myself, "Jeff, you're not going to procrastinate for the whole day." Ten minutes later, I was on the couch watching TV. I felt very frustrated at my many failed attempts, until I created this formula that I'm going to share with you right now. It's "*An Hour a Day Helps to Keep Procrastination Away.*" When I would wake up in the morning, I would have my daily self-meeting and I would construct my day. I would add in one hour without procrastination. I would pick out a time in the day, for example, 1 P.M. until 2 P.M., and for that one hour, I would force myself to work on any and all things that needed to be done. I would pay my bills, I would edit chapters, whatever. Gradually, after a week, I found that I was catching up on stuff I was very behind on. I began to enjoy these small personal successes and the next week I increased my hour by fifteen minutes. Within two months, I was doing three hours a day without procrastination. However, it wasn't as simple as it sounds. There were days where I fell back into the old pattern. If this happens to you, it's okay. Rome wasn't built overnight and kicking the habit of procrastination to the curb will not be simple. The really important thing to remember is, it's not how many times you fall, rather, it's how many times you get back up that will prove how successful you are.

I have provided some small exercises that I have used as motivation whenever I find myself falling back into the warm, comfortable blanket that procrastination provides. The first is a small self-questionnaire with two simple questions.

Exercise 1
Question 1
The first question is, "What is P-Diddy doing right now?"

You don't have to use P-Diddy. You can use anyone who has proven to be successful and truly a master in their field (e.g., Jay-Z, Donald Trump, or Bill Gates), someone you would strive to be like. Whenever I ask myself this question, the answer to the question is never, "Sitting on the couch, watching a re-run of *Pimp My Ride* that he has already watched once today." This question helps to remind me that to be successful, I can't be lazy and unmotivated. I can't sit on the couch and let my life pass me by or else I will never live the life I have always dreamed of.

Question 2
The second question is, "What is the person whose book may take my spot to be published this year doing?" If they're not wasting away hours, procrastinating while watching reruns and taking excessive naps, then I'm falling behind, big time. I must decide what is more important to my life: my career or my wasted moments? Obviously, you have to adjust the question so it applies to you.

Exercise 2
The second and very effective exercise is the sheet to beat procrastination. (If you read that correctly, it has a nice ring to it!).

This exercise will help you break your procrastination habit and help you to take a real major step towards success. You're going to either photocopy my sample, or make your own list like the one provided. The list will contain seven key questions.

You're going to stick this sheet all around your house in your favourite spots to procrastinate. If you only *read* this exercise, it will not work. It needs to be staring at you as a constant reminder to better yourself. This exercise is designed to force you up off of the couch or out of your comfortable bed. If done properly, this exercise is going to get you mad at yourself. You may even catch yourself pouting like a little kid. You may say stuff you haven't said in eighteen years, like, "But I don't want to get up," or "I don't want to do this," and yes, you may even say, "Do I have to?" How you answer these questions can make or break you.

Question 1
Who am I cheating by putting this off for another second?

Question 2
What will be the consequences for procrastinating for another second?

Question 3
How is this seemingly insignificant wasted moment going to affect my life?
(Believe me, all wasted moments eventually catch up to you.)

Question 4
What direction of a domino effect is this creating?

Question 5
Ask yourself this question again, but this time, with more emphasis:
"Who am I cheating by putting this off for another second?"
(Remember, you are only letting yourself down and allowing success to pass you by. Wasted moments create a domino effect, as well.)

You may begin to feel your body getting upset because it's realizing it can't procrastinate anymore. I found my brain would say stuff like, "Damn, I hate this exercise."

Question 6
"What is that person, who wants the same job, has the same goals or same anything as me, doing right now?" If they're not giving in to their laziness, you're falling behind, big time. Do you remember the story of the tortoise and the hare? The hare would have won and saved himself a lifetime of embarrassment, if only he hadn't procrastinated. I know this question is in both exercises, but I found it to be such a powerful question that I felt it needed to be in both.

Question 7
This time I want you to say it like I'm yelling it in your ear. "**WHO AM I CHEATING BY PROCRASTINATING FOR ANOTHER SECOND?**" Now, grab yourself up by the hair and finish whatever it is that needs to be done.

Goals
In this book, I talk a lot about goals and the importance of striving to reach them. So just what exactly is a goal? Goals are a life's driving force. Goals are what dreams are full of, and what a lacking life is empty of. Goals are usually the things you sit and daydream about during the day.

Accomplished goals bring a feeling of victory while lost and shattered goals bring the bitter taste of defeat. Goals are how you imagine you will look, feel, and act in the future.

They can be as small as a grain of sand or as large as the CN tower. Yet, with all that being said, you would be surprised at how many of us are really quite ignorant to something as simple as our own personal goals. This has never made sense to me. If you have no clue about what your goals are for your life, then what are you doing with your day? If you don't have a clear idea of what you're living for and what you're trying to achieve, then you are no different than a dog chasing its own tail. Ultimately, it is the goals we set and achieve that will have a large impact on who we become and what we do with our lives. The secret to achieving greatness is to set and reach great goals.

> *"Just because a man lacks the use of his eyes doesn't mean he lacks vision."*
> - Stevie Wonder

E = Mc Goal
I have good news for you. I have created a foolproof formula for reaching any goal you wish for in life. In math class, we were taught that showing the answer does not get you all the marks needed to

pass a test. You must also show your work. This same formula holds true for goal-setting. Listing a goal is a good start. However, without a formula for achieving this goal, you are only getting partial marks. To truly accomplish your goal, you must first come up with a plan of action on how to get there. I took my one-year goals and then rounded it down to the nearest number. I broke it down and split it in half. I broke it down further, into things I can do first on a daily basis which can help me to reach my weekly goals…which will help me to reach my monthly goals…which in turn help me to reach my six-month goals…which all eventually leads to my one-year goal…which helps pave the way towards my life's goals. Do you see the domino effect here? By creating a strong plan of action, you help to pave the way to success. You can't become a black belt in karate without first joining a karate school. Small goals lead to larger goals.

Visual Reminder

When I finally figured out my life goals, I found that sometimes I would fall off track. Sometimes I lost my drive. I had trouble staying focused on why I was working so hard. I realized that I needed a constant reminder of why I was making all of these sacrifices and doing all this hard work, so I created a visual goal board to illustrate what I was doing. I strongly suggest you create one as well. This goal board may seem silly, but the truth is that we have all become preoccupied with the idea of easy, instant gratification. That is why so many overindulge in television, drugs, alcohol, and sex: it is the instant gratification that these things provide that makes them so appealing. Working hard towards achieving your goals will be difficult. You may not see immediate results and this may force you to want to quit and take the easy way out, by picking up the remote.

Take this little exercise very seriously. It could be the difference in your life. I want you to get a large piece of Bristol board, just like the ones you used during high school presentations. Then, list all of your goals on this piece of Bristol board along with a picture of your goals right beside them. If you want to live in New York, cut out a map of New York, and stick it on your board. Anything you dream about must go on this board. Place these little, but powerful, words at the very top of your goal board: *"If it is to be, then it is up to me."* Truly, if these goals are to be accomplished, it is up to you to do it!

Then, take your visual goal board and stick it above your bed, where you will have no chance of missing it. Before you shut off your light and go to bed at night, I want you to stare at it for five minutes and imagine what it will feel like to accomplish all of these things. In the morning, when you lie awake just before getting out of bed, start your day by reminding yourself what you want out of life. Every time quitting seems like an option, go back up to your room and look at what you stand to lose by taking the easy way out.

Shooting Ourselves in the Foot
One of the worst things that you can do when creating a domino effect towards reaching your goals is to fool yourself into thinking it's okay to slow down and not work as hard as you have been. A perfect example is the person who quit drugs for a year, and then decides that he's going to celebrate his drug recovery by getting high. I'm sorry to say, but this person might as well just throw in the towel, because he has just killed his momentum.

When we start getting ahead in life, we tend to relax. We say things like, "I have done really well lately, so I can take a break or take the night off."

Once you stop momentum, it can be extremely hard to start it up again. Persistent actions will create life-altering results, whereas constant starting and stopping will create small and uncertain results.

Persistent actions are like climbing several large flights of stairs, two at a time. Constant starting and stopping is like going up the same flights of stairs, two at a time, and then stepping back down, one at a time, then stepping back up one stair, before then stepping back down two. You get the idea. While it is true that you're making progress, you're also wasting a lot of valuable time. You're retracing your steps over and over again. Who do you think is going to reach their goals first, the person who is going two stairs at a time the whole time, or the person who continues to retrace his or her steps over and over again?

This leads me to another familiar trend when it comes to how we shoot ourselves in the foot: I have never been able to understand people who create positive actions followed by negative, contradictory actions. I will give you a perfect example. People who go to the gym and run on the treadmill to lose weight, but then go home and eat an entire cake by themselves. The original action, of trying to lose weight by running on the treadmill, is a sure-fire way to start a domino effect for weight loss. However, the action of eating an entire cake afterwards robs you of any results created. If you want to reach your goals, take actions every day that get you much closer. Then reward yourself with positive reinforcements instead of ones that take away from your results. The best way to positively reward yourself is by asking yourself this question: "What is the best way I can reward myself for my hard work and dedication?" The answer I always find is more hard work and dedication.

Goals in All Areas
You would be surprised how something as simple as setting a goal and sticking to it can drastically change a life. The most successful people in this world are the most successful because of the goals they have set and accomplished. Goals come in all shapes and sizes and they also come in all aspects of life. Many people get confused and assume the only goals worth setting are the ones that bring in the most amount of money.

While it true that money plays a very important part of life, and that having a goal of being financially secure is a great idea, it's not the only aspect of life you should be focused on. Family and friends, and fun and pleasure should be some of the first goals that you ultimately want to reach.

> *"We tend to judge success by the index of our salaries or the size of our automobiles rather than by the quality of our services and relationship to mankind."*
> - Dr. Martin Luther King Jr.

Put Them Together and What Do You Get?
So, now that we know a little more about that nasty habit of procrastination, and we also know the importance of setting goals and a few ways to reach them, you may be wondering what the heck they have in common. Why would I possibly write a chapter about these two topics that are on completely different sides of the spectrum? The reason is because procrastination is to goals what kryptonite is to Superman. Procrastination is the one true killer of goals. You see, decisions will lead the way to your goals, but ultimately it's whether or not you procrastinate on the decisions you make, that will affect their ability to help you change.

Procrastination is the kryptonite to your dreams. It is the essence of unaccomplished goals and the reason behind failure. Nine out of ten goals never get accomplished because of procrastination. You can make up your mind all you want. You can do every exercise in this book. But none of it will help until you first decide to break the habit of procrastination. You are someone very important. You are the person who will make that ultimate decision on whether or not you are successful in life. You, and only you, are the person who can decide today to kill procrastination, or allow it to completely take over your life. By choosing procrastination over bettering yourself, you are only giving yourself permission to fail.

Keynotes to remember for Chapter 7

- Procrastination is nothing more than a habit.

- Goals are your life's driving force.

- Goals help to create success in life.

- The best way to achieve your goals is through constant and persistent action.

- Procrastination is the one true killer of goals.

Quote to remember

"Ultimately it is the goals we set and achieve that will have a large reflection on who we become and what we do with our lives. The secret to achieving greatness is to set and reach great goals."
- Jeffrey Moore

Workshop 7

Goals…

Goals…

Goals…

Goals…

Goals…

Workshop 7

Action 1
I want you to pick a goal, something small at first. Maybe it's to quit smoking for a week or to write the first chapter of your book. Whatever the goal is, it doesn't matter. Once you have chosen your goal, I want you to complete it. All too often, we start really strong and then as we near completion, we quit. Start a new pattern by choosing a goal and actually completing it.

Question 1
What is the goal for your life? If you don't know by now, I highly suggest you figure it out. Donald Trump's goal is to always be making the biggest deals. The goal of Dr. Martin Luther King, Jr. was to create equality. What is your life goal? One of the most frustrating things that I have encountered as I travel and speak to young adults is that they can name off all of their favourite reality stars' goals, but can't name any of their own. Create your own life and destiny by figuring out your life's goal.

> *"Nothing happens unless first a dream."*
> *-Carl Sandburg*

Question 2
What is the math towards achieving your life goal? I have already introduced you to the formula. Now, you create the results! If you have any questions about creating not only your goals but also your

dreams, the next chapter is the most guaranteed way to getting everything you want out of life.

Action 1
Create your own visual goal board.

Action 2
Photocopy or create your own question list for getting yourself beyond procrastination and into success.

Action 3
What one action have you taken towards overcoming a fear in your life?

Question 3
Have you figured out yet who the poisonous people are in your life?

Question 4
Are you still overindulging in Television?

Chapter 8
The Final Push Getting Naked with the Truth about Yourself, and the Six Fundamentals Towards Achieving Anything You Want in Life

"We are who we choose to be."
-The Green Goblin

This chapter is entitled "Getting Naked with the Truth about Yourself." In my mind, this chapter is the equivalent of taking a Black and Decker sander to your body and stripping away the layers of B.S. The goal for this chapter is to strip you down to your true self by peeling back the many layers of lies and excuses that you hide in. This chapter may hurt your ego and take a shot at your pride. With that being said, this is the most important chapter in the book. The fundamentals taught in this chapter have the ability to create a drastic and radical change in who and what you become in life. If you're still having trouble creating a domino effect for success, this chapter may be the answer you were looking for. None of the fundamentals will be new to you, as they have been talked about over and over again throughout this book. This chapter will demonstrate how to use these fundamentals together to create the domino effect you wish for out of life.

"Now all that is left is for you to become you."
- Sense

Fundamental 1

Become Your Own Leader

A major step towards creating success in any aspect of your life is to become your own leader. This means taking complete and total control of your life by eliminating the things that seem to take away from who you are. Becoming the leader of your life means taking back the control that you have unknowingly relinquished to others. It means taking back control over habits and maybe even, certain substances or people.

Look yourself in the eye and ask yourself this one question: "Who is really in charge here?" Are you leading your life or are you following? There is no yellow brick road in life to follow; we have to make our own way. Fill the shoes that you were born to fill and become the most important leader in your lifetime; **become the leader of you.**

> *"If you do not change direction, you may end up where you're headed."*
> *-Oriental Proverb*

If you are prepared to take this challenge and become your own leader, then you must come to the realization that you are responsible for exactly who you are, and what you have achieved and also haven't achieved up until this point of your life. Free yourself of any resentment, and relinquish any blame you may hold over others in your life. Ultimately, no matter what has happened in your life, it has been your decision to become exactly who you are today. If you are going to become your own leader, you must come to the understanding that you have either led yourself to this point of your life or you have followed. When I was sitting in my dorm room, eating three-day-old fries from a Taco Bell bag, I had an epiphany. I came to the understanding that I was living this life because I had allowed certain substances and people to blind me to my true potential. I allowed them to guide me into this situation. It was nobody's fault by my own for who I was then, and who I am now.

Every single day, we continue to take steps towards who we become. I didn't wake up this morning and just become me, and you didn't wake up this morning and magically become you.

Say it with me now, aloud: **"I AM RESPONSIBLE FOR MY LIFE!"**

One more time: **"I AM RESPONSIBLE FOR MY LIFE!"**

Ignite your inner fire and never allow anyone or anything to blow it out. Take complete and total control of your life today!

> *"Life will work for me when I realize...I am totally, completely, and fully responsible for what goes on in my life."*
> *- Lyanla Vanzant*

Fundamental 2
Eliminating Excuses and Creating Results

I once read that human beings lie because they are unprepared to face the consequences of the truth. This explains excuses to me perfectly, and why so many people choose to live through them. In life, the truth can hurt. Especially when it reveals us for whom we really are, and robs us from the lie of who we pretend to be. This next line could change your life. Excuses are nothing more than lies that we tell ourselves and others to justify not becoming who we thought we would become, and not working as hard as we should have to do the things we said we would. Please take a minute and read that sentence again.

It is much easier on the ego to sit back and create an excuse, than it is to look yourself in the eye and admit that you have lost your dreams due to your laziness and procrastination. Being lazy or being a constant procrastinator is the most arrogant and self-deprecating action anyone can take. To be lazy or to procrastinate and not work as hard as you can towards accomplishing the things you want most out of life, shows that you believe you are so gifted that you are naturally entitled to these things. It shows that you believe that life will just happen for you or that you just don't care enough to try. Either way, it will be your downfall; one day your little world will shatter and you will realize that your dreams have passed you by. You will come to understand emptiness that only wasted years, wasted potential, and a wasted life can bring.

In life, we can choose to live two different ways: We can choose to live through creating excuses, or we can choose to live through creating results. Those who choose to live through creating results, no matter what the adversity or challenge, will live their dreams. Those who choose to live through creating excuses will have plenty of daydreams. There is a common excuse that seems to be present in so many people's lives. In fact, nine times out of ten, when I speak to people about their vision or dream and why they haven't reached it, I usually hear this excuse: "I'm too young," or "I'm too old." It would seem that no matter what we wish to accomplish in life, we are never in the right age demographic to do it. I have always believed that we are all individuals, and that much like fingerprints, no two humans are the same. If this is true (and I strongly believe it is), then how can there ever be an appropriate age for anything? If death does not live by the age game, then why should we? You are never too young or too old to try anything in your life. There is no right age to try something new. There is no right age to go back to school. Live life and eliminate this or any other excuse that stands in the way of anything that you wish to accomplish. For every thing we wish to accomplish lies an excuse for why you cannot do it. So how do we eliminate excuses and create results? We do this through the third fundamental, which is dedication.

Fundamental three
Dedication
A vision is merely a daydream without action. When I speak about dedication, I want to make it very clear that I'm speaking on the action of dedication, and not simply the word, "dedication."

They are not the same thing, so please do not get them confused. Actions always speak louder than words. This is especially true in today's society where words seem to be completely silent and meaningless.

Here is a perfect example: I could say that I'm truly dedicated towards writing a book. However, if I show my dedication by sitting on the couch procrastinating and overindulging in television, then I show my dedication to be merely nothing more than a word without action. True dedication means constant and persistent action towards reaching a goal. It means that there are no wasted moments. One day of dedication is a good start, five days of dedication is even better, and twenty-five days of dedication is a complete waste of your time if, on day twenty-six, you decide to quit.

> *"We are what we repeatedly do. Excellence then is not an act, but a habit."*
> *-Aristotle*

Remember that quote, because it is so true. *"We are what we repeatedly do."* For us to create a result with anything in life, we must first create an action. A perfect example of this would be you couldn't read the words on this page without first taking the action of opening the book. In life, ultimately it is our actions that have the biggest say in who we are and what we accomplish. How many times in your life have you already said, "I would love to try that," and yet, have never even taken one single action towards actually getting any closer?

You cannot accomplish anything in life without first taking an action.

Be very aware of the actions you make every day because they will ultimately have the final result in what you accomplish in life. Now that you have come to the understanding that actions create results, you must also come to the understanding that we are in constant action. Everything we do is an action that creates a result, and thus a domino effect. Sitting on the couch procrastinating and watching TV is an action that will create a result.

Picking a goal and working as hard as you can towards achieving it is an action that will create a result.

I really need to hammer this home: ***Whatever it is that we do on a daily basis will ultimately have a result on what we achieve in life and who we become.*** That last sentence is so important. If you have a highlighter, please highlight that sentence, because it is the absolute truth. In life, we are either doing something or we are not.

The most empowering words in the English language are "**I AM**," because if you are, then you are, and if you're not, then you are not. There is a huge difference between saying you are doing something and any other words you can find. If you are not doing the things in life that you need to be doing towards creating success, then you are doing the things you shouldn't be doing, that will rob you of it. Before everything you do in life lies these three little letters: **I AM**.

The people I admire the most in life are the ones who have the courage and the absolute brilliance to take the proper action towards reaching their dreams. These people are few and far between. Most people never muster up the courage to take action towards achieving the things they want most out of life. Most people would rather wonder than ever actually know.

> *"Lack of action is the creator of excuses."*
> *- Jeffrey Moore*

A perfect Example of Eliminating Excuse and Creating Results Through the Action of Dedication
When I set out to write this book, I made an early decision not to overindulge with other people's success stories. Sometimes hearing other people's successes can only dampen our spirits. Sometimes success stories don't motivate us and only make things worse; they can help to remind us that we haven't yet reached the level of this

person. If there is one success story I want to truly focus on in this book, it's yours. This book was created so you could write the pages of your own personal success.

That being said, I do feel it is necessary to speak about one person's success in life that is truly an inspiration to me. He demonstrated that it's not what happens to a man in life, but rather what he does with it, that truly shows his sense of worth and true character. This man is an example of what being a leader, eliminating excuses and creating results through the action of dedication can do. I want to tell you a story of a fellow Canadian, one who makes us all proud.

Terry Fox had just graduated high school when he lost his leg to cancer. Losing a major appendage at any age can be extremely traumatic, especially when you are a teenager. Terry took this major blow, not as a setback, but as a personal challenge. He did not sit on the couch feeling sorry for himself, nor did he sit there and ask, "Why me?" as I'm sure many of us would. He stayed physically active and became a world-class wheelchair basketball player, before switching his focus to running.

In 1980, cancer research was poorly funded. Terry decided he was going to change this. He accepted his own personal challenge and began training every day, running at least twenty-six miles a day. As a result of his intense training, Terry's prosthetic leg would cause him to sometimes bleed. He suffered from bone bruising and extreme shin splints. But he never quit. On April 12, 1980, Terry Fox began his adventure to raise money for cancer research by running across Canada. The Marathon of Hope would start in Newfoundland and end in Vancouver. He dealt with much frustration as he received little media coverage in the early stage of his endeavour. He persisted though, never losing sight of his true goal: to raise money to help fight the battle that forced him to lose his leg.

While running, Terry came up with his ultimate goal that he would try to raise one dollar from every Canadian to help fight cancer. As his run continued, the media picked up on his story. He was soon on magazine covers nationwide and was talked about every day in the news. Terry made it through Newfoundland, Quebec, and deep into Ontario before being forced to stop. The cancer that had stolen his leg had now spread to his lungs. Terry's act of leadership to force a change in the world eventually raised over 24 million dollars that year; essentially one dollar from every Canadian. Terry had run 3,330 miles in just 143 days. His passing was a national day of mourning in Canada. To date, the Terry Fox Foundation has raised over 200 million dollars towards cancer research. Terry Fox, one of Canada's greatest sons, is a true example of what asking a better question can do for you. Terry, you will always be remembered.

Remember, if you're always looking for the reasons why you can't, you will never find the reasons for why you can. I hope you will remember that statement and keep it with you whenever you're in doubt about the possibility of your own success.

> *"Circumstances do not make the man – they reveal him"*
> *- James Allen*

Fundamental Four

Hard Work & Sacrifice

Hard work and sacrifice are very important actions that we must take to create success. Hard work and sacrifice are the actions that many people choose to create excuses for not doing. We all live in our comfort zones, and hard work and sacrifice is what can rip us out of these zones.

Why is it that so many actually fear these two actions? Stepping out of our comfort zones and attacking life is a guaranteed way to achieve success. When we step out of our comfort zones and into a new realm, we begin to discover what we are capable of. The more we continue to push ourselves, the more we discover what we are made of, which leads to growth. You may not realize it but you are very set in your comfort zone and your way of life. The major problem with comfort zones is that we get too comfortable with how things are.

Example

We all have those mornings where our beds are the most comfortable they have ever been and we actually risk being late for work or any other appointments so that we may indulge for five more minutes. However, staying in bed and over-indulging in comfort creates a result of running behind. I don't know what its like for you, but when I'm rushing, I seem to miss important details, like a spot while shaving or wondering if I left a stove element on, which clouds my focus all day and leads to me being frustrated. Do you see how a small, insignificant thing like taking five extra minutes of comfort can create a domino effect? Now imagine if we stayed in bed an extra five years! This might sound ridiculous to you. But when was the last time you made a drastic and radical change with your life? How long have you been overindulging in your comfort zone? If you want to see how set you are in your ways, sacrifice something you do on a daily basis for forty days. It must be something major. Giving up something small will not prove anything. The amazing thing about the forty-day challenge is if you take away something major, for instance television, alcohol, or makeup, you would quickly see just how set you are in your ways. The reward from this challenge is the growth you will receive from it. If you take something you never thought you could live without, and then actually live without it, you will radically change what you thought you were capable of and who you thought you were. I don't want you to think that is the only part of hard work and sacrifice, because believe me, there is more. Sacrifice means giving up the things we would rather be doing short-term, for long-term accomplishments and results. When I wrote this book, I sacrificed many things. One of my sacrifices was partying. I knew that partying would bring me nothing more than short-term happiness. After the night was over, I would be no closer to completing this book than I was the night before. Five years from now, I won't be proud that I went out and got drunk with the boys. I will, however, be very proud of the hard work and sacrifice that I put towards creating this book. Sacrifice means giving up the things you like for things you love, to accomplish the things you truly do love. To be truly dedicated means sacrificing short-term pleasure for long-term gain.

> *"When things go wrong, don't go with them."*
> *- Anonymous*

Fundamental Five

Self-Question

The most important conversations you have in your life are the ones that no one else ever hears. Your self-conversations are often created from your self-questions. From the moment you open your eyes in the morning, your brain begins asking hundreds and hundreds of questions. In fact, your brain never rests, and throughout the day, your brain is constantly searching for the answers to the questions you are asking. Be very aware of the questions you ask because nothing can kill your self-esteem like a negative answer created through a negative question.

Different Approaches

There are two very different approaches to self-questions.
There is the negative, "Shoot yourself in the foot" approach, which so many fall victim to every day, and is great for killing self-esteem. Or, there is the positive approach, which really helps to pick you up when you're down and gives you something to build on. Here is a small list of common negative self-questions:

Negative Questions
- Why me?
- Why am I not good enough?
- Why do I always fail?
- Why does every one else have it better than me?
- Why can't I just have everything I want?
- Why do I even try?
- Why do I even bother?
- What's the point of trying?

Do you see how these questions can really kill your self-esteem? These are the self-questions usually asked by lazy, unmotivated people.

Below, I have provided a small list of positive questions. Can you see the difference, not only in the approach, but also in the answers they may provide?

Positive Question
- What can I do to improve upon this result?
- What must I master to improve my results?
- What lesson am I failing to learn in defeat?
- What am I prepared to do to create a better result?
- What have I learned from this?
- What am I prepared to do next time, to improve my result?
- What am I doing constantly to create this result?
- What approach can I take next time?
- What did he do to get the result that I want?
- Who can I talk to about this situation?

Do you see the difference between questions? Negative, self-pitying questions come across as whiny and weak, whereas positive questions come across as strong and empowering. By asking "why me?", your brain may produce an answer like, "Because you're a loser." However, by asking "what can I do to improve upon this result?" your brain might come up with an answer like "Study and work harder and you can achieve." Negative questions produce negative, self-limiting answers. Positive questions produce answers which will provide you with the most empowering solutions.

> *"It's hard to beat an enemy who has an outpost in your own head"*
> -Sally Compton

Fundamental Six

Believing in Yourself Through Failure

There is absolutely no doubt in my mind that if you decide to use these fundamentals that they will undoubtedly lead you to failure!

That's right. You read those words right! The problem with failure is that there is a misconception almost everyone has regarding what failure truly is. Many people view failure as a failure, when in reality failure is nothing more than a progression towards success. You see, for true success to exist, failure must also exist! They are the yin and the yang; one cannot exist without the other.

Michael Jordan didn't make every shot and Mozart didn't play all the right notes. But what these two individuals did do was to never allow a failure to stand in the way of their ultimate success. Every time you fail, you are actually being taught a lesson for how to achieve success next time. I guarantee that when you where much younger, at one time or another, you probably stuck your hand under hot water and quickly learned it burned. As we become older, we become much less receptive to the lessons being taught to us every day.

Instead of lessons, we see mistakes and personal sabotage that stop us from a life we want and deserve. Mistakes are what we need to learn from to continue to move further ahead and evolve into successful people. We are continually burning our hands and not learning to use the cold water. Take a past failure in life and turn it into a lesson.

> *"Insanity is doing the same thing over and over and expecting a different result."*
> *-Albert Einstein*

Failure is nothing more than a stepping-stone on the way to climbing the mountain of success. The only time that failure is actually failure is when it is followed with these words: **"I QUIT."**

We all have the ability to truly become great at something. Inside of us lies more potential than we ever dreamed possible. In fact, if we were to look our potential in the eye, it would blind us.

I have come to realize, that in twenty-five years from now, when I'm forty-eight years old and I'm looking back at this point in my life, I don't want to say these words: *"I wish I would have..."* I am not prepared to look back on my life and feel regret. How long in life are we prepared to say the words *I wish* before we actually begin to live?

> *"If you think you can, you can. If you think you can't, you're right!"*
> -Mary Kay Ash

There is absolutely no doubt in my mind that if you take these fundamentals seriously, you can drastically change your life. There is no doubt in my mind of this, because it is through these fundamentals that I have created the most powerful domino effect I could ever ask for.

Never Forget!
Over the seven months it took for me to write this book, there were many times I wanted to quit. There where many times when I wanted to be out drinking and partying instead of sitting at my dining room table, hunched over a laptop that froze every fifteen minutes. Looking back, I regret nothing, and all of the sacrifices were worth it. It's in our weakest hours that the temptation of quitting turns into a real possibility. It is our weakest hours that tempt us to take the easy way out. It is in our weakest hours when we must learn to be the strongest. It is when I catch myself saying, "I want to quit," that I know I mustn't. To me, there is no greater waste than someone who is just average. Average people are just people who allowed themselves to quit at being great. If I can change and be successful, then there is no question in my mind that you can too. Recently, I slipped. I fell back into my old behaviour. This is not hard to do. Living a life of just not giving a shit and partying can be very tempting.

I had fallen right back into my old domino effect without even realizing it. I was getting drunk, partying, and doing drugs all the time again; I had lost sight of my true goal. I had become a hypocrite and did not deserve to be the author of this book. I lost my real focus and replaced it with one of a much lesser value. If there is one thing I have learned, it's that true change is a lifelong battle.

The important thing was that I caught myself before I got out of control. In your attempt at bettering yourself, you will slip and you will fall. The key to success is catching yourself before you fall in so deep it's almost impossible to get back up. You are what you surround yourself with; a lesson I have learned the meaning of, once again.

> *"For all sad words of tongues or pen the saddest are these: It might have been."*
> *–John Greenleaf Whitter*

My Last Words
Here is what I know after twenty-three years on this planet:

I know that the only way to live is to be happy and to spread love.

I know that we are all on this earth in search of each other.

I know that if you have never lived it and experienced it firsthand, then you have no right to pass judgment or criticize.

I know the best way to find love is to let it find you.

I know the best thing to be is yourself.

I know that there is always a glimmer of light, no matter how dark it seems.

I know that today turns into tomorrow, and fades into yesterday, in the blink of an eye.

I know that hard work today will equal success tomorrow.

I know that ignorance is ignorance, no matter what.

I know that someone will always have it better (and worse) than me.

But most importantly, I know that every step taken is one step closer than I was before, no matter what direction I take it in.

At the risk of playing off the immortal words of John F. Kennedy, I will close with this:

"Ask not what your life can do for you, ask what you can do for your life."

Good luck with your life, domino effect, and success.

> *"Man is not fully conditioned and determined, but rather determines himself whether he gives into his conditions, or stands up to them. In other words, man is ultimately self-determining. Man does not simply exist, but always decides what his existence will be, what he will become in the next moment. By the same token, every human being has the freedom to change in an instant."*
> *-Viktor E Frankl*

Keynotes to remember for Chapter 7

- You are solely responsible for your life.

- You have led yourself to this point.

- Excuses are nothing more than self-lies.

- Dedication means constant and persistent action towards reaching a goal.

- Action always speaks louder than words: What are your actions saying about you?

- There are no wasted moments in true dedication.

- Hard work and sacrifice are essential in achieving success of any kind.

- Negative self-questions produce negative self-answers.

- Positive self-questions produce positive answers.

- Failure is nothing more than a progression towards success.

Quote to Remember

"Every step taken is one step closer than you were before, no matter what direction you take it in."
 - Jeffrey Moore

Workshop 8
The final push…

Your Final Workshop

Self-reflection 1
You did it! Good for you! You should be incredibly proud of yourself for making it this far. Congratulations for completing this book and not giving up.

Exercise/ Action/ Question 1
This is the most important question in this book and the reason this book was written.

What will you do with your own personal domino effect?

The greatest gift I could receive is for you, the reader, to move beyond what you once ever thought was possible and accomplish your goals and achieve the life you have always dreamed of. I have left some contact information in the back of the book and hope that you will contact me and tell me all about your domino effect. Thank you for your time and allowing me to express how I feel.

Prove it
You want to be successful? Prove it!

You want to be the best? Prove it!

You want to be respected? Prove it!

This book was written in the hopes of waking you up to your true potential. All the words to read have been read, and it is now on you, the reader, to go out there and prove what it is you want so badly in life. How badly do you truly want it? I have listened to many who say they wanted something badly, but when it came to action, they never even lifted a finger. You want it? Go out and get it. Show the world what you have to offer. Show the people who have said you could never do it just how wrong they are. Open the eyes of the world with your personal shine. Blind the nay Sayers and conquer everything that lies in the path of your dream. This is your life: Take control and live it to the fullest! Remember, it won't be easy and you will have setbacks; there are no mistakes, just lessons learned. And remember, the domino effect for success lies squarely on your shoulders and no one else's. I truly believe we all have the talent and skill to propel us to anywhere we want to be in life. We don't all have the same dreams because we don't all have the same lives. So enjoy the one you have!

In setting out to write this book, my only aim was to create something I truly cared about; something I felt represented me to the fullest. I didn't feel it was necessary to drag out this book longer than it needed to be. I have noticed many authors feel the need to take what would have been a great book and stretch it out to fill a quota of pages. Sometimes less is more. I also wanted to be sure that people truly felt they could commit to reading this whole book. Congratulations on completing it! You should be proud of yourself. For some people, it may be the first book you have fully read since high school. For others, it may be the most recent of many. Whatever category you fall into, I want to thank you for choosing to stick with me.

"If you only remember me as a boy, then you will never see me as a Man"
- *Jeffrey Moore*

Twenty_Something_in_the_Twenty_Somethings@msn.com

Printed in the United States
69823LV00004B/169-183